Shades of Meaning

Shades of Meaning

Comprehension and Interpretation in Middle School

Donna Santman

HEINEMANN
Portsmouth, NH

Heinemann
A division of Reed Elsevier Inc.
361 Hanover Street
Portsmouth, NH 03801–3912
www.heinemann.com

Offices and agents throughout the world

© 2005 by Donna Santman

Library of Congress Cataloging-in-Publication Data
Santman, Donna.
    Shades of meaning : comprehension and interpretation in middle school / Donna Santman.
        p. cm.
    Includes bibliographical references and index.
    ISBN 0-325-00664-4 (alk. paper)
    1. Reading (Middle school).   I. Title.
LB1632.S35 2005
428.4'071'2—dc22   2004024883

Editor: Kate Montgomery
Production: Elizabeth Valway
Cover design: Night & Day Design
Composition: House of Equations, Inc.
Manufacturing: Jamie Carter

Printed in the United States of America on acid-free paper
09 08 07 06 05 RRD 1 2 3 4 5

For Adi, who, at twelve months of age,
has taught me that a rich imagination has powerful rewards

Contents

foreword
New Images of Teaching, New Images of Reading

Donna Santman's classroom is full of the energy of people trying to get smarter, to do better, to reach for more than they will yet grasp. Situated in lower Manhattan, with a view of New York Harbor and the Statue of Liberty, this school takes in the pulse of life and energy of its environment and harnesses that to students' development of literate lives. Its excellence, however, is not a product of geography; this is craft—the craft of an inventive and questing teacher. Donna has, with *Shades of Meaning*, given us the gift of a look into her wonderful classroom and her mind as a thoughtful and highly professional teacher.

We live in a time when there is much public discourse about teacher quality and high standards for students. Most of this talk is Orwellian doublespeak, as in "war is peace, slavery is freedom, ignorance is strength." The words "teacher quality" have come to mean reducing the requirements for certification to the passing of a single test. "High standards" for students, likewise, have been reduced to the kinds of thinking, reading, writing, and doing that can be easily tested—and thus the meaning of the words "high standards" have been turned upside down. This book, in contrast, is a study of the struggle of having truly high standards, ones that keep getting higher as life and learning continue. For Donna, caring about the quality of students' reading means remaining unsettled about how things are at the moment. It means sometimes pushing students at moments and in ways they do not necessarily want to be pushed. It means thinking hard, as a teacher, about one's own words and behavior in order to ask for more from kids. Living with high standards is a struggle, and it is serious work. Achieving high standards means having a well-developed teaching craft.

As Donna tells her story of helping students get better and better as readers, she lets us watch her teaching from backstage, as it were, and we have an opportunity to observe some of her stagecraft. I want to attend, first, to what she does externally and materially as she teaches, and later, I will discuss some of the thinking and planning that inform this work. Reading involves thinking, and teaching reading involves externalizing thinking so that students can participate in it with their teacher and later internalize it. Donna provides accounts of many conversations with her whole class, and in each of these conversations, she is looking for a way of externalizing some complex behavior. Often, she reads aloud and then talks about what she is thinking, how she is making sense of what she reads. Sometimes, she uses tools, like sticky notes or charts or writing, and when she does, the tool has a clear purpose—externalizing some kind of thinking so that the kids will be able to try the same tool with a similar intellectual purpose. Her use of a projector allows both the text and her use of tools to be visible to the class; afterward, students apply the principle of the tool to their own book, in private, or with a partner. Typically, the students move from watching a demonstration, to participating with a large group, to participating with a partner and less teacher guidance, to using the strategy on their own. In this sequence, there is a gradual transfer of responsibility from teacher to student, a handover of the reading strategy. Donna's purpose is not just to have a good class discussion today, and it is not for everyone to leave with the same understanding of the shared text under consideration. The text and the tool are means of learning ways of reading that should last each individual student the rest of her or his life.

Watching the dance of bodies during these stages of activity is instructive. We see the students dispersed at first, and then Donna calls them together. They assemble, with their notebooks, around the overhead. We see them look at her, as she speaks and acts animatedly in front of them. They jot some things down. After a while, they scoot into pairs, to try out something with a partner. Donna kneels and moves from pair to pair, interrupting, redirecting, and extending. She returns to the front and summons them back together, at which point some individuals report or ask questions. She dismisses them to their independent work, and they disperse again, this time all over the room. She takes her clipboard now, and circulates among them, talking to them individually or in small groups. There is, through this sequence of moves, a shifting back and forth of who goes to whom, who takes information from whom and writes it down. And there is a suite of social arrangements with varied degrees of support. Intellectual learning—heady stuff—happens through very specific movements of bodies in space.

Because a handover of responsibility is at the heart of her teaching purposes, many of the instructional scenes are situated in one-on-one conferences with readers. Between whole-class lessons, students read books they have chosen. They bring to these books their interests, their reasons for choosing them, some expectations of what the book will have in it, and all the knowledge and experience that fuel those interests, purposes, and expectations. The fact of their intention eliminates much of the need for pre-reading activities, background about the text, or other such apparatuses to which many teachers assume they must attend (and for which they must prepare). Therefore, the teaching focuses on what the students are doing right now in order to have the fullest possible experience of the text. We see Donna, again and again, asking her students hard questions and pushing them to do more intellectual work. Anyone who thinks teachers let go of intellectual rigor when they work with students who are reading young adult literature they have chosen should read carefully these stories of conversations between readers and their mentor. A new kind of rigor becomes possible when the teacher focuses not on the excellent elements of a shared text but on the habits of mind that are characteristic of excellent readers.

But how does a teacher know the habits of mind characteristic of excellent readers? Donna draws upon a habit of watching herself as a reader, and using what she learns from such self-observation in her demonstrations for students. Ultimately, each of us, like Freud, must create a model of mind based upon our own experience of our own minds. To that, we add our empirical observations of students and perhaps some empirical observations of other insightful teachers and researchers. But we return to what mind looks like from the inside in order to imagine the kinds of thinking we will externalize for students.

Donna does research her students. We see her, early on, getting her tools ready for assessment in just the way a researcher must organize data collection. She must be ready to take students in—to see them as they are, to understand what is going on, to make theories actively about what she sees, and to act upon those understandings. And as she turns each curricular corner, she does so on the basis of what her students are doing, what they do and don't understand. Often, we watch Donna become bothered or a little disappointed by what her students are so far able to do. She examines her own expectations and makes a plan from there about what she needs to teach in order to move her students to greater strength. We hear much, these days, about research-based instruction, and most of the talk is, once again, doublespeak and deception. In this book, readers have an opportunity to observe instruction that is much more solidly research-based than most of what bears that label, with a much higher degree of validity. The teacher-researcher is on-site, forming instruction on the basis of data that are appropriate to the setting and individuals in that setting.

Researcher habits of mind are the most useful tools for assessment and accountability. Legislators and policy makers are enamored of these words, but they are a long way from understanding what they really mean. Reading about Donna's constant, systematic assessment of her students, her clear communication of her high expectations, and her relentlessness about holding students accountable for quality work, I cannot help but be struck by the irony that sometimes, all of this is interrupted so she can prepare students for state "assessments." Tests do not add assessment, accountability, or standards to this classroom. Compared to the daily work, the imposed tests look like puny things, barely worthy of note, except for the damage they can do to students' conceptions of themselves as learners and to their life chances if their scores are low. An atmosphere of accountability is a product of relationships—kids' relationships to people who are significant to them. It is not created by strangers in bureaucratic offices or by part-time scorers in some other state. Donna's descriptions of her conversations with these kids she loves remind us of how it feels to be in a relationship where participants expect great things from each other.

This relationship involves both participants being visible to each other and each participant feeling known by the other. Throughout this book, Donna describes the ways she plans her teaching in order to adjust something that students are doing. Then, they overdo the new thing, so she has to adjust again and teach in order to mitigate the distorted effects of her prior teaching. Teaching is dialogue, as assessment and instructions represent opportunities for each party, student and teacher, to speak and be heard.

Shades of Meaning is about helping readers understand how active they need to be, on several different levels of thinking. Comprehension, interpretation, and critique involve the reader putting something into the reading event, something that is not present in the text itself.

Let's consider a very small example. Read this little quote, which has been attributed to Vaclav Havel (though I cannot confirm the source):

> Vision is not enough; it must be combined with venture. It is not enough to stare up the steps; we must step up the stairs.

We will consider this a little text, though it must have come from a larger one. These two sentences appear with most things left out, and we have to do some work to figure out what they must be talking about. Even the larger text, though, would not be completely explicit. No text says everything it means. Writers have to make decisions about what they will put into their texts and what they will leave out, what will be made explicit and what will be left for readers to fill in. No text (or utterance in speech) is explicit; listeners and readers always must participate in restoring what is missing or filling in implications.

So in order to read the little Havel text, we must do some work. Reading "vision is not enough," we have to hold open a couple of possibilities for the word *vision*. It could be the literal sense of sight, which would make it likely that after the semicolon, the rest of the sentence might have to do with other senses that must supplement vision. Or it could be "the vision thing" of politics or leadership, the notion that those who lead must have some grand sense of direction and purpose. It is not until we get to *venture* that we can start to narrow the possible meanings. Since *venture* does not create a parallel about physical senses, we assume we have pinned down the second meaning for *vision*. It must mean something like *a hope and plan for one's world.* But this use of *venture* is a little unusual. In the United States, we would usually use that word as a modifier for the word *capital*, or perhaps for a certain kind of journey. It has something to do with going outside the normal route and taking on some risk in some way that requires some effort. Then, surprisingly, the first part of the next sentence has to do with *staring* and *steps.* This does not follow in any literal way the thought we were just considering about venturing. Vision, we came to understand, was not a literal and physical thing because of the way Havel used the word *venture.* But now we're back to staring. He's moved from abstraction to something more concrete. We have to bring knowledge to bear, knowledge about how language usually goes, about metaphor (though we do not need to think that word in order to use this knowledge). The steps are a metaphor, a concrete symbol for the abstract idea in the first part of the quote. Now that we are thinking metaphorically, we are operating on two tracks— envisioning a concrete image and also interpreting an idea. We must activate what we know about steps and stairs. We probably use some mental image drawn from our experience, and we also know that stairs are steps, that they require some effort, that sometimes people find them difficult. At the same time, we must make that image work with the first part of the quote, the part about vision and venture. We could analyze dozens of separate acts of meaning that come together in a single, instantaneous act of reading, ones that expert readers do without even realizing they are doing it, but ones that are sometimes mysterious for some students.

Readers must bring their memory of experience to a reading event in order to make the text live in their minds. They must activate their understanding of language, of human intention, of what is likely to occur in the physical world, to infer the meanings of phrases and sentences. They must use their assumptions of what people are like to attribute motivations to characters and understand what is going on in narrative scenes. They must connect their understandings of this text to many other texts in order to develop interpretation, a sense of how this text is saying something into the great human conversation. And they must compare the claims of this text to the world they know in order to critique its assumptions or challenge the existing world. From literal understanding through the interpretive to the critical, readers must restore missing elements, must co-author what they read.

Many readers will recognize what I have been describing as *transactional theory*, which, in the world of reading, owes the most to Louise Rosenblatt. Rosenblatt is often understood as emphasizing mostly the role of the reader as a participant in creating meaning with text, and in fact she did emphasize that contribution. But she also emphasized that the reader does not accomplish this in a bubble. The text constrains the possible meanings a reader can legitimately make, even as it is open enough to permit the reader to work and create.

In earlier chapters of *Shades of Meaning*, Santman pays particular attention to the work readers must do in order to allow the text to constrain their thoughts, that is, readers' work to attend to what a text actually says. This is close work in the transaction between reader and text, and I often imagine Donna as a kind of border patrol. Usually, border patrols are associated with limiting movement across borders, enforcing separations. What Donna does, however, is to make sure borders remain as open as possible and that there is sufficient movement across them. Textual information needs to move into the reader and the reader needs to act upon that textual information in order to co-create the literary (or informational or political) experience. The text needs to have sufficient impact on the reader's attention that the reader can be transacting with a relatively stable *something*. Otherwise, there is no dialogue. The text cannot "listen," and the reader is not listening either; each is isolated from the other. For a transaction to occur, the reader must occupy at least two different positions: she must speak for the text and speak for herself. She must make sense of what the text is saying (thoughts she could not have made by herself) and also make an answer in response to the text. Understanding can consist of nothing less.

Such a view of reading still, even at this late date, contradicts much of what is common in school practice. The institution of testing still reinforces the dominance of a view of reading as a transmission, an assumption that meaning moves from the page into the mind. In such a model, the assumption is that the teacher is responsible primarily for clearing brush from the pathway so that information can move smoothly without getting tangled. That readers are actively doing something, using their unique experience and knowledge in order to make sense of text, even at the level of comprehension, is still a radical thought in many settings.

Santman's practice, then, will be challenging to many teachers and administrators, but they will find that it repays their efforts. We cannot help students grow as readers by simply insisting with more and more fervor that they *just get it*. We have to learn ways of opening the process to them, sharing with them the strategies common to successful and passionate readers. In the process, educators may find themselves teaching students to attend more carefully to evidence that is right in front of them, to make meaning of that evidence actively and assertively, to develop theories about how the evidence addresses important issues in the world, and to act upon those theories in order to improve things around them. Such habits of mind are bigger than reading. There are worse ways to spend one's time and energy.

Randy Bomer

Acknowledgments

This book grew out of more than a decade of teaching, beginning in the fall of 1992, at the Bronx New School. I am forever grateful to Mimi Aronson for introducing me to the world of reading workshop and for believing in my ability to become a workshop teacher. I am thankful also to the students in my first class, in particular Fitawrari Mangasha, who helped nurture a novice teacher and revealed to me the joys of teaching.

Of all of the people who have inspired me as a teacher, I am most indebted to Randy Bomer, for showing me that reading critically and teaching critically can transform young minds. I first met Randy when I had the great privilege of working in one of the most rigorous learning communities education has to offer: the Teachers College Reading and Writing Project. I am thankful to Lucy Calkins, founder of the project, for her dedication to learning and for providing me with constant opportunities to rethink my own teaching. I am also thankful to the members of the Upper Grade Reading Think Tank, in particular Kathy Doyle, Ann Marie Powers, Erica Denman, and Kathleen Tolan. Their classrooms have always helped me envision what's possible for my own.

When I decided to return to the classroom after spending some time as a staff developer, I searched for a school that would support my beliefs about reading and writing while at the same time challenge those beliefs in ways that would push me to grow. I found that school in I.S. 89. Ellen Foote, who created the school and still serves as its principal, is a true educational leader and the most thoughtful and provocative principal I've ever known. I've benefited greatly from her guidance and nurturance. To my colleagues at 89, especially 89 pioneers Joel Spengler, Alex Lee, and Stacey Peebles, and literacy department members Jess Goff, Audra Robb, Jenny Bender, Christina DiZebba, and Lis Hamilton, thank you for your patience and willingness to reimagine your teaching year after year. And to my students, whose stories make up the bulk of this text, I am genuinely humbled by your thoughtfulness and thankful that you have been a part of my life.

I have been incredibly lucky over the years to have spent time in the company of powerful educators across the country who have pushed my thinking beyond what I could have imagined. First and foremost, I am eternally grateful to Gaby Layden, without whom this book would not have been written. I am thankful for her patience and willingness to listen as I struggled through each and every chapter. Many of the ideas in this book have grown out of conversations with Kathy Collins, Katherine Bomer, Ellin Keene, Mary Ehrenworth, Ellen Spears, Claire Noonan, Isoke Nia, Lisa Ripperger, Katherine Casey, Ginny Lockwood-Zisa, Johanna Cohen, Lydia Bellino, and Laurie Pessah. I am thankful for their insights.

I am also blessed to have spent time in the classrooms of wonderful teachers across the country whose generosity and hard work have been an inspiration. I am particularly grateful to the teachers at Lanier Middle School in Houston and at Roosevelt Middle School in San Diego, who took on this work with a fury and reminded me that communities of teachers working together can transform schools.

My editor, Kate Montgomery, has been a constant source of encouragement. I am grateful for her belief in this book from the very beginning and the wisdom she offered along the way.

My parents, Rae and Don, and my sister, Andrea, have always inspired me and I am grateful not only for their support of my writing but more importantly for helping me take time off from writing when I needed a break. My cousins Evelyn and Ed Lieberman have always believed in me, and I am thankful to them for showing me how to live a life dedicated to giving back.

It's traditional to thank one's spouse for allowing one the time to write or providing much-needed distractions when the writing gets too hard. Incredible thanks, however, goes to my Danny, the greatest husband the world has ever known, for *pushing* me to write. The rigor with which he works has been a model and a challenge, and I am so grateful for his loving support.

Shades of Meaning

....

Chapter 1

Imagination

It's inevitable that whenever I tell people, "I teach middle school," they look at me with great sympathy.

"I'm so sorry," they say, or "How courageous."

"No," I respond. "I like it."

And it's true. I like working with kids at a turning point in their lives, when their greatest hope is to be taken seriously and understood by the adults around them. It makes me laugh to see them argue against conformity after having colored their hair pink because that's what everyone is doing these days. I find strength in their ability to rethink their actions and beliefs when faced with a compelling reason to do so. I share the excitement they feel at those "aha" moments when they make connections with their worlds and admire the loyalty they show their schoolmates and friends when fighting against a perceived injustice.

But, despite their ability to be compassionate and insightful, all too often, middle schoolers can be melodramatic and thoughtless. This was made painfully clear recently when I popped my head into the office of my principal, Ellen, to say goodnight and she told me about Caroline. Apparently, that afternoon, Caroline had cut her drama elective and spent the period crying in the girl's bathroom. After a long talk with the guidance counselor, she revealed that the night before, she had discovered a posting on a website with all sorts of gossip about her. Everyone had been talking about it that day. Caroline felt humiliated, but even more troubling was the fact that she felt there was nothing that she could do about it. The damage was done. Her life was over. She might as well just hide from everyone and cry.

An hour and a half later, Ellen and I were still talking, but we were no longer talking only about Caroline. We were also talking about how challenging it feels to teach middle schoolers, whose priorities are more often the dramas of their peer relationships than their schoolwork. We talked about how the kids' concerns feel small and insular, and how the students rarely see any possibility for change. It's as if they can't imagine anything or anyone beyond themselves. The world is a fixed space and they feel powerless to turn the challenges they face into something positive.

Ellen and I have had this conversation before. We have often talked about how our school needs to help kids understand new ways of thinking and acting that will allow them to see possibilities in their lives and in the larger world around them. We challenge the conventional wisdom that kids will be kids and that this is just a phase they will eventually grow out of. We believe that it is our job to help the kids grow into healthy and thoughtful participants in society. We believe school curriculum should be designed to do just that—to help kids *imagine* a life beyond what is immediate and see themselves as activists in building that life.

The potential is there. My colleagues and I have witnessed and participated in enough class discussions to know that many kids have hopes and dreams for a better world for themselves and their communities. Too many kids, however, are resigned to accepting conflict and bad feelings. They don't believe that the way they think, speak, and act can make their lives and the world around them different.

Ellen and I ended our conversation by agreeing to reexamine how curriculum can help kids think and act differently. For myself, this meant looking closely at how my literacy curriculum teaches kids not only to read with strength and power but also to use reading as a way to imagine themselves as strong and powerful.

Defining Imagination

What does it mean to imagine? Most of us at some point in our lives (perhaps on New Year's Eve or on the occasion of an important family milestone) have tried to *imagine* what our lives would be like five, ten, or fifteen years ahead. Sometimes this requires us to resist what others think is our proper or expected future. Instead we try to see that which is outside our immediate vision and dream up new identities and opportunities for ourselves. We read beyond the text of our lives to create a world larger than the one we are given.

As teachers, when we convey ideas about imagination in school, however, they are rarely connected to any reality. Instead, kids are said to have good imaginations when they make up impossible worlds—when they create characters and situations that border on the ridiculous. "Imaginative" kids write plot-driven murder mysteries or rock star stories that go nowhere. They aren't interested in developing thoughts and opinions about the books they are reading because it interrupts the story. In the world of imagination, there's no conflict, no ideas being explored. Yet, because the characters are from a made-up time and place, or because they use fantastical weapons or have skills that are inhuman, the stories are described as imaginative.

Imagination, however, can be more than this. Instead of developing an imagination as an end, we can use them as a means, a path to something better and larger than ourselves. Using one's imagination with rigor and power can even be the difference between life and death. Shortly after September 11, 2001, we often heard the word *imagine,* but it was used as an excuse. Did we know enough to predict that this terrible crime would be committed? Was the intelligence sufficient to suggest such a possibility? When the 9-11 Commission released its report to the nation, it was the commission's declaration of a "failure of imagination" rather than the failures of intelligence that was in the lead of every news story. *New York Times* columnist Tom Friedman (2004) pointed out that Americans, or more specifically, the Bush administration and the intelligence community, never imagined that terrorists would hijack airplanes and use them as bombs to blow up the World Trade Center and the Pentagon. But, he argued, had they read the clues carefully and powerfully enough, they might have been able to imagine such an atrocity—and three thousand people might have been saved.

I believe the core of our mission as teachers is to teach kids to develop and then use their imaginations in more powerful ways. If we show them how to think beyond the "intelligence" of the classroom, perhaps they will be ready to participate in creating a safer, more positive world.

Reading as Imagining

Reading is one of the strongest ways to develop imagination. Reading can introduce new answers to conflicts in our lives. Reading can help us take responsibility for injustices and inequities around us. When we read, writes Judith Langer (1995), we imagine horizons of possibility for ourselves. Good readers envision the world of the story in our mind's eye. We teach this understanding to our kids when we teach them to make pictures in their heads as they read. But instead of limiting our instruction to helping kids make pictures of the world of the *story*, we can also teach them that they can use the story to help them make pictures of their own worlds, and thus imagine new possibilities for their own lives and the lives of those around them.

And it's not just any reading. There's a particular kind of reading that allows kids to develop this proactive imagination. For a long time, my greatest goal as a literacy teacher was to get kids to simply love reading. I wanted them to choose to spend their free time curled up with a book. I spent lots of time teaching them how to read for long periods of time without interruption. I taught them to picture the story in their mind's eye, to laugh and cry with the characters about whom they were reading.

But reading to develop an active imagination involves more than just getting lost in the world of great stories. If they read carefully and thoughtfully, and pay attention to the details of the books they read, our kids will be able to explore the big issues and ideas in their lives. This kind of reading will help to inform decisions about the work they'll undertake and the friends they'll have. Reading this way helps us decide who we'll vote for, where we'll donate our money, how we'll treat people. When we teach kids to read this way, they will learn to harness their imaginations and use them to accomplish great things.

CHAPTER 2

Reading Workshop
A Place to Cultivate Imagination

Reading curriculum that develops thoughtful and imaginative civic participation requires a particular kind of teaching. It doesn't just happen because we let kids pick up books of their choosing when they finish the work we've assigned. And it doesn't happen when, at the end of a year consumed by comprehension strategies, we tack on a small series of lessons that focus on reading for social action. It needs to be central to the curriculum. We must explicitly teach kids that as they come to understand what a text is about, they can also come to understand the following:

◆ There are issues and ideas hiding in the texts they read, and their job is to name those ideas and think about how they are explored across texts.

◆ The world is complex and we can use reading to develop the ability to see connections between seemingly contradictory ideas.

◆ There is great value in explaining one's thinking thoroughly and at length.

◆ The big issues in the world— such as race, class, and gender— are not black and white. Seeing these ideas as complex and inter-connected involves attending to the details.

◆ Reading can help us believe we have the power to act on our new understandings and can therefore change our current situation.

This kind of teaching should not be reserved for a few select lessons; it should be the foundation of our reading curriculum. It requires us not only to teach strategies for critical reading but also to create structures in our classrooms where kids can self-initiate those strategies. For me, as well as thousands of teachers around the country, that teaching is embodied in reading workshop.

Reading workshop is not a curriculum, but a set of teaching structures and practices that give kids the opportunity to bring their reading lives into the classroom for the purpose of stretching themselves in the company of others. The reading workshop format allows me to explicitly demonstrate the strategies and habits of mind employed by critical readers. And it has provided the kids I teach with enormous opportunities to practice reading, thinking, speaking, and acting in response to their new learning.

Structures of Reading Workshop

The Minilesson

Reading workshop is structured so that the bulk of the time is spent pursuing the work of reading. It begins with a short lesson in which the class, as a community of readers, gathers together in the meeting area. I teach a strategy that I want the kids to apply to their reading. I might put a text on an overhead and demonstrate for them how I pay attention to markers in a text that reveal shifts in characters' attitudes. Or I might put up a sticky note a student has written to serve as a good example of developing a thought about the ideas hiding in a book. I never teach them about the *text*, but rather about a strategy for reading the text.

The kids take notes on the minilesson in a literacy notebook and perhaps try out the strategy a little with a shared text or with their own reading just to get a feel for it before they go off to work independently. In the workshop, kids use the strategies as they need them while they are reading. On any given day, kids may be using that day's strategy or drawing on strategies taught in the past. The expectation is always that kids are engaged in the unit of study and are letting the minilessons affect the way they read.

I am careful not to turn the lessons into assignments that students have to do on the day they are introduced.

Independent Reading and Conferences

Once the minilesson is over, the kids go off to pursue their own independent reading, either alone or with partners. They read books of their own choosing—books they can and want to read. They get these books from the classroom library, which is always open to the kids and has a clear system for checking out and returning books. I have designed the classroom library to meet the needs and interests of the students but also to help them consider books they might not otherwise choose. It contains fiction, nonfiction, poetry, and magazines and is organized for easy navigation. Some books are grouped by genre or topic or difficulty; others are lined up spine out in alphabetical order by author's last name. I also make displays around the room of books I want to highlight—perhaps books that I've recently brought in, or books that don't seem to be circulating, or, most often, books with subjects that will help students explore issues that matter to them.

During the work time, as kids are reading, I make my way around the room, clipboard in hand, to confer with the readers. During a conference, I assess the student and determine something I can teach him or her as a reader that day. More often than not, I use conferences to demonstrate how imaginative readers think. I document the content of the conference on a record sheet I keep on my clipboard. The record sheet is a chart with a space for each kid in the class. This allows me to see whom I've had a conference with and whom I need to get to. I carry with me not only the current chart but also old charts so that I can refer to notes from previous conferences as I work with the students. Each day I confer with five to seven students. This allows me to get to an entire class in a little over a week.

The Closing

At the end of the work time, the kids and I gather back in the meeting area for a closing to the workshop. Typically, I share something I've noticed about the way they've been reading or cue them to something they need to be thinking about or working on as the unit progresses. For example, I might tell them I've noticed that a lot of them are starting to choose books more critically. Or I might tell them I've noticed that many of them are having a hard time trying to interrupt their reading to think about the symbols in the text and that they should be prepared for a minilesson the next day that will address their struggles.

Units of Study

None of the minilessons I teach sits in isolation. Each is tied to a larger unit of study in which we are engaged, which is organized around a large idea about reading that I want to explore with the kids. These units of study build upon each other across the year, and each one helps kids strengthen their capacity to use reading as a tool for developing their imaginations.

When I was a new teacher, I struggled with planning for my teaching. In fact, in those days, I thought workshop teaching meant you couldn't plan ahead and that all the lessons had to come from the kids. I'd pull alongside a kid for a conference, and whatever he was doing that seemed important for the rest of the class to know would become the next day's minilesson. One day we'd learn about retelling, the next, what to do when you don't know a word, and the next, how to develop ideas about the characters.

Of course that made for very messy, very unaccountable teaching. I have since come to understand that workshop teaching should, in fact, be carefully planned. Because there is no teachers guide to follow, no formal scope and sequence, teachers of reading workshop need to create curriculum plans within their communities. Therefore, I spend a portion of each summer developing an outline of my curriculum for the entire upcoming year, which I bring to the first faculty meeting in the fall.

Like the plans made by most teachers at my school, my curriculum outline shows a year divided into units of study. Each unit of study is anywhere from about three to eight weeks long and explores a particular idea about reading. I write out these unit ideas in full sentences to force myself to fully think through what I want the kids to understand about each. I organize the units so that they will build on one another and carry my class on a journey of learning.

Should the reading ideas I explore in this book be organized into a curriculum outline, it might look like the table below.

I've planned this particular curriculum because of the context in which I teach. I am the eighth-grade teacher in a 6–8 school that embraces workshop teaching in all classes. Kids come to my class already having experienced reading workshop. They already know how to choose books they can and want to read and have strategies for making their way through books. They come to my class already armed with some strategies for talking and thinking about their reading.

If my kids were more disenfranchised as readers, either because they came from a different kind of teaching and learning experience, perhaps one that organized its curriculum around literary analysis of a whole-class novel, or because reading was not a part of their lives, I might begin in a different place. I might not start with personal connection. I might start with learn-

GUIDING CONCEPTS

Good readers try to see themselves in the books they are reading and therefore make a greater investment in their books.

Once we are more invested in our books, we feel more compelled to make sure we understand them by attending to more of the text.

Readers understand that there's more to a text than the words on the page and know that understanding a text involves some figuring out, or inferring.

We can think about how we will read a particular text. We understand that people who want to use reading as a lens through which to think about society know that there are issues hiding in their books and can develop strategies for naming and thinking about those issues in well-developed interpretations.

It is the details and what we make of them that help us think about the issues that are in our books. Our goal is to think about them in interesting ways so that we can deepen and develop our imaginations.

ing how to negotiate the library and choose appropriate books. Or I might start with teaching kids that reading is about more than just understanding what's happening in the story and that they can actually develop thoughts and opinions about what's going on in the story as they read. Whatever way I begin and then let the year unfold, however, I am always focused on moving toward teaching a kind of interpretation that allows kids to connect their reading to the communities in which they live.

Developing Strings of Minilessons

With these reading ideas as guiding concepts, I continue the outline by developing strings of minilessons that will demonstrate for kids the strategies involved in reading in these ways. Because workshop curriculum is responsive to the needs of the particular group of students in front of us, it is impossible to plan each and every lesson in advance. So I tend to plan a series of lessons that will open up the idea we are going to explore, then during work time I search for patterns of difficulty and turn them into follow-up lessons.

For example, during a unit of study organized around helping kids understand that good readers try to see themselves in the books they are reading and therefore make a greater investment in their books, I might plan to include lessons in which I demonstrate making personal connections when we read. I might teach kids that characters can remind us of people we know and that we can come to care for those characters as a way of thinking about our own relationships. When I send the kids off to work, I might discover that lots of them are struggling to do more than just name

Guiding Concept	String of Minilessons I Plan For
Good readers try to see themselves in the books they are reading and therefore make a greater investment in their books.	◆ Demonstrating how to let characters remind us of people we know ◆ Learning to let characters help us think about our own relationships

those connections. Therefore, I might develop follow-up lessons in which I teach them to develop some thoughts and opinions about those connections.

Assessment

Right from the start, as I begin planning units of study, I think about assessment by asking myself, "How will I know the kids are getting it?" This design model, suggested by Grant Wiggins and Jay McTighe in their book *Understanding by Design* (1998), has been transformative. It helps me determine the follow-up lessons for any string of lessons. It also holds me more accountable to keeping my unit on track and to making sure my teaching is as clear and explicit as possible.

To figure out how I will determine whether my kids are understanding what I am trying to teach, I consider the following issues each time I plan a unit of study:

- ◆ defining what good work looks like
- ◆ developing a system for collecting information
- ◆ designing artifacts for formal assessment

Defining What Good Work Looks Like: Making Learning Outcomes Visible

I must be able to describe in words familiar to my students what it looks like when they are doing the work competently or when they're struggling. I need to know what it looks like when they're almost there or when they've gone beyond expectations. In my classroom, like many others, this defining takes the form of a rubric. I create a rubric for each idea about reading that I plan to teach. I use this same rubric to evaluate everything the kids do in a particular unit of study. I use it to think across conferences, to look at students' reading notes and charts, and to listen in on book talks. My kids use the rubric when they reflect on their growth as readers after every unit.

For example, in a unit of study on helping kids develop interpretations, the rubric might look like that on page 13.

Criteria	Meets Standard	Approaches Standard	Exceeds Standard	Area of Concern
Demonstrates the ability to negotiate justifiable interpretations.	Is able to find provocative ideas in reading and negotiate those ideas across the book in compelling ways.	Is able to think about an idea, but the idea is not particularly provocative or compelling.	Is using all the predictable questions to stretch thinking and develop new ways to think about books that take into account the complexity of the issues.	Is able to name an issue, but then talks only about the book's surface-level content.

On the left side of the rubric is the unit's guiding understanding. Here, my expectation is that students can develop interpretations that are justifiable. I define a justifiable interpretation as one that is interesting, convincing, and accountable to the text (see Chapter 8 for more on interpretations).

The language used to state the degree to which the student meets the criteria is written across the top of the chart. In this case, if a student's work meets the criteria, she is considered to have met standard. If her work is almost there, she is determined to be approaching standard. If her work is beyond expectation, she exceeds standard. If she is struggling, this work is considered to be an area of concern. Because the goal of the class is to get everyone to meet standard and *then* exceed it, "Meets Standard" is the first column on the chart. "Exceeds Standard" is third because most kids begin the year approaching standard, then grow to meet the standard, and finally exceed it.

Under each category is a description of work that fits into this category. The language used to describe each is created out of the language of the classroom. I tend to develop a rubric about a third of the way into a unit, when we have created some ways to talk together about the topic. Using this language in the rubric helps make the assessment more explicit and accessible to the kids.

Developing a System for Collecting Information

In order for conferring to be a supportive assessment tool, I need to take notes about my conferences. Most importantly, these notes must be organized so that I can see each student's progress across time and make sure that no one falls through the cracks. Some teachers I know like to carry a binder around with a section for each student. In the front of the binder they might have an attendance list. After each conference, they not only fill in notes in that student's section but also cross that student's name off the class list. I carry a clipboard around with a class chart that I fill in as I make my way around the room. On any given day, I can see whom I have and have not conferred with during that round of conferences. I also keep a stack of earlier charts with me, so I can see a record of each student's progress over time.

I also need to have a system for reviewing notes. There's no reason to write anything down if I'm never going to look at it and yet, if I never look at it, how will I remember what I taught in previous conferences? Reviewing my notes every week allows me to see patterns in student work that I can turn into future curriculum. Additionally, these notes become tools by which I can evaluate student growth and become concrete evidence I can present when I meet with parents.

Making Teaching Stick: Creating Artifacts That Can Be Formally Assessed

Reading workshop is a textbook-free method of teaching and learning. This is powerful because it forces us to learn both about reading and about the students in front of us in order to teach them. But it is also challenging. One of the greatest challenges is that our students often seem like Teflon—our teaching just doesn't stick to them. So often, when we teach a lesson and just send the kids off to pursue their own independent work, it's as if the lesson didn't matter. We pull alongside kids for conferences and they repeatedly tell us, "Oh, I'm just reading." In response to this lack of engagement with our lessons, we begin to require that the kids try the strategies. But too often these strategies become mindless assignments to be completed rather than tools the kids can reach for in the midst of their ongoing reading work.

One way to make students' reading processes and progress more visible is to create a variety of artifacts that will help me see into the kids' thinking as they are reading. In my classroom, these include literacy notebooks, newsprint charts, and self-reflections.

Literacy Notebooks

One way that I've tried to make my teaching stick is to expect that kids will take notes on the minilessons in a literacy notebook and will have that notebook out during work time. The notebook is just a two-subject spiral book.

One section is reserved for notes from writing lessons and the other is reserved for reading notes. The kids also keep any artifacts from their reading in this notebook. These artifacts include

- sticky notes from books they've finished, arranged on clearly labeled pages;
- charts and diagrams they've created to extend their thinking about a text;
- thinking they've done about the read-aloud;
- notes connected to conversations they've had in partnerships or book clubs; and
- lists of texts they've read.

We use the notebook in a variety of ways. One is during conferences. I've made it a regular habit to make the notebook a part of my reading conferences. I often ask kids to page through their notebook and look for notes or artifacts that they think could help them do what they are trying to do. We also use the notebook to reflect on our growth as readers. We make it a regular habit in each unit of study to reread our notes and artifacts and talk about what we notice about how our reading has changed across this study. For example, during a unit of study on making more of the parts of the books we are reading, students might reread their artifacts and notice that early on in the unit they would develop a thought about a character or situation in the book and leave the thought as it was. Later in the unit, however, they were able to trace the ways in which characters changed and developed simply by continuing to make more of the characters' words, thoughts, and actions.

The literacy notebook also allows the kids to deepen their thinking about the ideas they are exploring because they have to document that thinking in an organized way. One move we often make when we are working on an idea is to look through our notebook for other times in our reading when we were thinking about this same idea and then try to think between the two, or connect them. For example, when Dina was reading Robert

Cormier's *Chocolate War*, she found herself thinking a lot about power. By way of extending her ideas, she reread her notebook and found that power was an idea she thought about across a number of texts, including George Orwell's *Animal Farm*. By looking at her *Animal Farm* notes, Dina discovered that power is gained and maintained in different ways. This move also allowed her to examine power structures in her community.

The literacy notebook has been a great way to communicate with parents. On a regular basis, I ask kids to give their parents a tour of their notebook and talk through what we've been learning in class as a homework assignment. That is, the kids go home and sit side by side with a family member and describe the lessons I've taught and how they've begun to incorporate those lessons into their own reading. In a textbook classroom, the textbook is often the tool by which parents find out what their adolescents are learning in school. Without a textbook, there's a void. A well-kept literacy notebook fills that void.

These notes and artifacts make the literacy notebook a great product for assessment. Therefore, every two weeks, on an assigned day, kids turn in their notebooks and I assess them according to our rubric.

Newsprint Charts

For years I've watched my colleagues in the math department use newsprint as a tool for helping kids work collaboratively on math investigations. I'd walk into any math classroom in the building, and more often than not, kids would be sitting side by side in front of a piece of newsprint on which they were doing their math work. The paper would be filled with diagrams and newly discovered algorithms and words describing their strategies. The newsprint helps kids collaborate by giving them the space to think and work through a problem together. It also allows the kids an easier way to share their thinking with others.

I've recently brought newsprint into my literacy classes. I began by introducing it in conferences with reading clubs. When I saw a group struggling either to sustain a conversation or to develop an idea, I offered them a piece of newsprint and some markers. I told them that the newsprint was just a tool they could use to improve their conversations. Their job was first to get some ideas down and then to see whether they could organize those ideas in a way that could expand them. By that I meant that they could re-make the ideas into a diagram or a chart that would allow them, through comparison or reorganization, to see new possibilities.

At first, I noticed that kids were simply using the newsprint to record ideas they had already shared. But with a little conferring, the groups began to see that they could use the paper itself to extend their ideas. For example, groups who have a hard time sustaining a conversation now have a tool to anchor their talk. Simply by putting a topic in the middle of a page and brainstorming ideas in the form of a web, kids who felt they had nothing to say suddenly have a lot more ideas. And their goal of trying to fill up the page helps them think of more to say. Along with offering the groups another strategy to support and extend their thinking, the newsprint offers me yet another artifact that reveals what kids are able to do.

Self-Reflection

Strong learners see learning as recursive. That is, it doesn't move forward in a steady line but loops back over itself and accumulates. And strong learners build into their learning opportunities to step back and think about how they have grown and what goals they might create for the future. The workshop classroom is an important place for such reflection. Periodically throughout the year, I ask kids to reread all their old work and reflect on how they've grown as readers. Sometimes that reflection takes the form of a general "Dear Donna" letter. I invite the kids to tell me about an aspect of their reading lives and to think about the changes they've made. For example, for an end-of-marking-period assessment, I've often asked kids to write me a letter explaining how they think they've grown over the marking period. In one letter, Brian wrote that since our unit of study on making more of the details of a text, he found himself getting through fewer books in a certain period of time. He continued by writing that he thought it was good that he was reading more thoughtfully, but he worried that he was not reading enough. This letter allowed Brian the opportunity not only to step back and reflect on his reading but also to develop some plans or goals for the future. The reflection also gave me a window into what Brian thought was important in reading and how he felt he was doing.

Other times I give kids a more formal sheet that asks them to respond to a series of open-ended questions, such as How has our study of learning to read with critical concepts affected your own independent reading? When I ask the kids to respond to these questions, I require that they do so with specific examples from their reading. I don't want a simple reiteration of my minilessons, but a chance for them to really think about the intersection of teaching and learning.

Reading Materials

Planning for my teaching involves thinking about not only the understandings around which I'll organize a unit and the lessons I'll teach to develop those understandings but also the materials I'll teach from and make available to the kids.

Most importantly, I want to make sure that I help kids understand that thoughtful, critical, imaginative reading doesn't matter just when we read literature. Therefore, it is important to design a diverse classroom library and to gather materials for demonstration that cut across all genres—novels, trade books, magazines, poetry, short stories, picture books, and so on.

Central to my library, however, is young adult literature. This genre, developed over the past twenty years, has provided me with an essential context within which to help kids explore personal concerns and consider experiences outside of their own. And while I sometimes struggle with the extent to which the stories focus on bleak and sensitive topics, I do value the diversity of experience and identity represented in the material.

Young adult books are not just part of the independent reading library but also central to my teaching. When I demonstrate a reading strategy or habit of mind to the kids by putting a text on the overhead, it is often a short story from a collection of young adult literature. When I read aloud to my classes, more often than not I read young adult fiction.

Other Teaching and Learning Structures

The final part of my planning is concerned with the structures in which we'll do this work. I always provide time for kids to read independently in the classroom, but there are also a variety of other structures I can use that will support kids in developing these reading understandings.

Read-Alouds and Literature Discussions

When planning curriculum, along with independent reading, I consider the role that read-alouds and literature discussion will play in the unit. Regularly across the week, my kids and I gather together for a read-aloud and a book discussion. This is a time for us to develop our ability to talk about books. I read the text aloud to make it accessible to all students and to model fluent, engaged reading.

I consider a number of issues when I choose a read-aloud. I look for something that will engage the kids as well as open them up to new reading and thinking experiences. I read aloud from a variety of genres so that kids will see that I value diversity in reading and so that I can demonstrate expressive reading with many different kinds of texts.

More often than not, I read aloud a short text—a short story, an article, an essay, or a poem. I make this choice because of the time limits of a middle school class. When making choices about how to use my forty-minute reading workshop, I keep in mind that I want kids to spend most of their class time reading their own books. This means that I typically read aloud once a week, sometimes twice. Perhaps once a year, I take on a novel, usually when students are in reading clubs and need to develop more strategies for discussing a book over time.

Talk is one of the most important mediators of learning we have in the classroom. Through class discussion, kids are forced to give shape to the ideas that swirl in their heads. They are made to push those ideas out of their mouths for others to hear. They are given the opportunity to hear and respond to ideas from their classmates, ideas they might not have considered before. In this way, talk becomes a fundamental tool for helping kids imagine new worlds for themselves in the classroom.

Throughout my teaching (and throughout this book), I offer strategies to help kids talk effectively about their reading for the purpose of articulating and thinking through their interpretations. It is most important to establish right from the start, however, that classroom discussion is controlled by the kids. They decide what's worth talking about and who will talk. That does not mean I am absent from the talk. It means that instead of offering up topics for discussion by presenting questions to the class, I teach them ways of finding ideas that are worth exploring. And instead of controlling who talks and how the ideas develop by calling on kids who raise their hands and responding to each student comment, I let the kids carry on a conversation. They simply know they can talk when no one else is talking and they have something to say about the ideas we are exploring. In this way, the kids are accountable to each other. They are accountable for making themselves understood and making sure they understand each other. They are also accountable for thinking rigorously and presenting information that is accurate and appropriate to the conversation (Institute for Learning, University of Pittsburgh 2001).

Collaborative Reading: Partners

At various times in the year, my students also gather in different collaborative reading structures. As mentioned earlier, kids sometimes read with partners. Some of these partnerships are informal, perhaps forming as two kids reach for the same book in the library or find themselves talking about similar reading interests and decide to read together. Other times, these partnerships are more formal. That is, every kid in the class might be in a partnership that practices the strategies we've been discussing in class. For example, they might meet in partnerships a couple of times a week to read through a short text together and practice saying the text aloud in a way that makes it make sense. Or they might meet in partnerships to practice strategies for interrupting their reading to develop thoughts about a text along the way. These partnerships, while balanced out across the week with plenty of time for independent reading, provide the kind of support and accountability often needed to get kids to stay engaged with the texts they are reading.

Collaborative Reading: Book Clubs

In addition to partnerships and often later on in the year, when kids have more experience reading and talking together, we form reading clubs—long-term groups of four to six kids whose goal is to read and discuss many books and ultimately to build a reading history together. This reading history allows each individual in the group to deepen his or her ability to think not only "inside of" a book but also across books. When a group builds history it creates more intertextuality. More intertextuality—more looking across texts and letting one text get you to think about others—allows for more well-developed, more nuanced thinking. It is this complexity of thought that allows kids to find new ways to see, think, and act in the world.

Step Back and Reflect

Throughout the past twelve years, as I've worked to develop a reading workshop that is rigorous and engaging for my students, I have relied on many master educators around the country whose books have helped me imagine what's possible in my own teaching. The following books have been essential to helping me turn my room into a place where reading matters.

Randy Bomer and Katherine Bomer, *For a Better World: Reading and Writing for Social Action* (2001)

Lucy Calkins, *The Art of Teaching Reading* (2001)

Ellin Oliver Keene and Susan Zimmerman, *Mosaic of Thought: Teaching Comprehension in a Reader's Workshop* (1997)

Frank Serafini, *Lessons in Comprehension: Explicit Instruction in Reading Workshop* (2004)

....

CHAPTER 3

Real Assessments of Reading
Finding a Direction for My Teaching

Uncovering Reading Secrets

At the start of each school year, I typically ask my students to complete a reading questionnaire meant to uncover the role that reading plays in their lives. At first, I asked them to tell me about the books they loved and when and where they chose to read. While the answers were somewhat helpful, the questionnaires always fell short. They never yielded the kind of information that I could really use to figure out how to teach the kids to read more powerfully.

Recently, I decided to make a change. Instead of asking questions about their general reading lives, I decided to start in a more sensitive place by asking the kids first and foremost, "When do you fake reading and why? That is, when do you act as if you are reading and really aren't, and when have you said you've read a book that you haven't?" It may sound strange to begin the school year with such negativity. After all, the beginning of the school year is usually spent building community, getting to know each other as readers, and imagining the kind of year we will create together. But this is middle school, and one thing I've learned about middle schoolers is that by the time they get here, most of them have mastered faking it—faking reading, faking community building, faking school. If I had any hope of changing that, I knew I needed to start with uncovering their reading secrets.

I introduced the questionnaire with a discussion of honesty in reading workshop. I wanted the kids to understand that in this class, the only right answer was the one inside their heads. They should forget trying to figure out what I wanted them to write and just write what they were thinking. Then I handed out the questionnaires and sent them off to work.

That evening as I read through their responses, I found that by far, most of my ninety students had faked reading at one time or another and many faked on a regular basis. This did not surprise me. Many kids claim to be reading books their teachers have assigned, but in fact aren't. They simply follow along with other students or ask their friends what happened in the assigned chapters just in case the teacher calls on them. Some claim they might fake reading assigned texts if the teacher requires them to read too many pages in too little time. Other times kids fake reading when they feel pressure to read a particular number of books. New York, like some other states, requires that students read twenty-five books per school year. Students chose books that they can and want to read. They read the books during independent reading workshop and at home. Students' completed texts are documented on a book list that is checked periodically during the year and recorded on report cards. Many students, feeling pressure to keep up with reading, put on their lists some books they haven't read. The cleverest of them list books they've read in previous years, just in case their teachers question them.

Additionally, for many kids, the books chosen for whole-class novels are simply too difficult and it is easier to just pretend to follow along with the class and get what they can from class discussions. This is schoolwork, after all. Many feel that all they have to do is get a decent grade. Many of the kids do not see reading as something that has to do with them personally, let alone as a way to imagine what's possible for their lives. Those who do, do not see school reading as something connected to the reading they do in their personal lives.

If I had any chance at pushing out the boundaries of their reading and getting them to reimagine the role reading could play in their lives, I knew I needed to change these attitudes.

Looking at Reading: An Early Assessment

First, however, rather than make assumptions, I wanted to learn more about what the kids actually did when they had a book in their hands. In years past, I would begin this part of my reading curriculum with an assessment that would allow me to match kids to books they could and wanted to read. But an assessment aimed at helping kids find books they can read independently doesn't really focus my attention on seeing what kids are doing when they are struggling and the ways they compensate when they are confused. So this year, I decided I would add another assessment into the mix. This year I would try to see more of what my kids were doing as they were reading—what it looked like when they could do it and what it looked like when they couldn't.

Looking at research into proficient readers and studying critical literacy helped me come to the following understandings about strong readers:

- Strong readers can *envision*—they can build the world of a story in their minds (Keene and Zimmerman 1997; Langer 1995; Pearson et al. 1992).

- Strong readers can *read between the lines*—they can construct not only what literally happens on the page but also see the deeper meaning behind the words. They understand that often the literal words imply more, and they try to ask questions that allow them to unpack the belief systems a text suggests (Bomer and Bomer 2001; Edelsky 1999; Keene and Zimmerman 1997; Langer 1995; Pearson et al. 1992).

- Strong readers can let a story lead them to *develop big ideas* about the world of the story and, by extension, their own worlds (Bomer and Bomer 2001; Edelsky 1999).

I decided to create a context to see these qualities in action. I did so in order to figure out how the kids in my own classroom read. I wanted to understand what was happening when kids could read all the words on the page but had no idea what the story was about. What did the reading sound like? What was going on in their minds? I wanted to understand what was happening when kids could understand the plotline of a book but weren't reading between the lines and figuring out the deeper meaning of the text. I wanted to understand how kids were turning their understandings of a text into larger interpretations—into bigger ideas about the world of the text and possibly their own worlds. And I wanted, finally, to get a sense of whether the kids were developing thoughts and opinions about those bigger ideas. Were they simply naming ideas that developed across their books, or were they also able to think about those ideas in relation to their own experiences and understandings?

In order to find out whether or not these processes were happening in their reading, I needed to find just the right story. I was looking for a story that would expose different aspects of reading. M. E. Kerr's "Do You Want My Opinion?" (1985) was just that story. "Do You Want My Opinion?" is a short story included in Donald Gallo's collection *Sixteen: Short Stories by Outstanding Writers for Young Adults.* It is about a world that at first seems very different from ours. In Kerr's world, people regularly kiss and engage in public displays of affection. Young people are encouraged to "stick to lovemaking" and told that "nice kids" don't share their thoughts. Intimacy is defined not as physical affection but as the sharing of thoughts and opinions. Kerr's world helps us see the social norms we create as community constructs and invites us to reconsider our norms by telling a story that turns them on their head.

In the story, John, our protagonist, is desperate to share his opinions of Chinese-American relations, the situation in the Middle East, and a variety of other current issues. Instead he regularly sticks his head under the cold-water faucet. The story begins in the morning just as John is getting ready for school. His father wanders into his room to give him "the lecture," warning him not to get too intimate with Eleanor Rossi. In other words, he shouldn't ask her opinions. John heads down for breakfast wondering when was the last time his parents shared an opinion. He can't imagine they ever shared their thinking, even though he knows, in fact, they have. John walks to school with Edna O'Leary, and like the others in the school yard, they cuddle each other. Once in the school, he goes into the bathroom for a smoke and while gazing at the drawings of heads on the bathroom wall, he thinks of Lauren Lake and her comments in Thoughts class the week before. Mr. Porter had asked the class for a definition of dreams and Lauren had raised her hand and told of a dream she had had about a world where you could say anything on your mind, but you had to be careful whom you touched. This provoked quite a bit of laughter and nervousness in class—so much so that Mr. Porter ran back and kissed Lauren. John thinks that maybe he's just like Lauren. He wants to tell people about the books he's read and what he thinks about history. Nonetheless, he puts the memory out of his head and leaves the bathroom. As he swings through the door, he sees Lauren heading right toward him. He has to do everything he can to stop from blurting out questions about science and literature. But he instead kisses her.

To prepare for this work, I developed a list of ideas that I would use as criteria through which to examine the kids' reading, and I developed a system for conducting the individual assessments. First, I wanted to confirm for myself that the kids could get every word right and still miss the story, so I asked the kids to read the first page to me out loud. This also helped me understand more about how fluency affects comprehension. Then I wanted to know that they could build the world of the text in their minds, so I asked them to retell the story, focusing on what happened first and then next and so on until the end of the story. I had chosen a text that would require kids to understand that there's more to a story than what's literally on the page and that to read well often means to figure out what's not there. To know more about whether and how this was happening for kids, I asked them to share with me anything they had figured out about the story. Lastly, to get at their emerging sense of interpretation and their ability to develop an interpretation, I asked them to share with me any bigger ideas they thought the story evoked and to consider their own personal opinions of those bigger ideas.

With the text and my criteria in hand, I spent the next two weeks trying to see what I could discover about what my kids were doing as they read.

"DO YOU WANT MY OPINION?" NOTES

Criteria	Comments
Retells the story fully.	
Figures out the story and develops bigger ideas.	
Has thoughts and opinions about the bigger ideas.	
Reads aloud with fluency and accuracy.	

Each day, after a minilesson on using the library or strategies for developing stamina as a reader, I sent the class off to read and asked a small group of students to read "Do You Want My Opinion?" independently and meet with me individually. Throughout our time together, I documented everything the kids said on a record sheet that outlined the criteria.

Patterns of Misreading

As the days passed, I became more and more amazed by the patterns I was seeing. Over and over again I watched the kids read and miscue in the same ways. I knew that to name these patterns would be to figure out how to angle my teaching. It's important to note here that I did not use this research to determine the individual reading abilities of my students. I didn't try to create levels or categories of readers. It is impossible to determine the reading ability of each student from one classroom reading experience. And while I did discover particular concerns about some kids and decided I would need to do plenty of follow-up work with them, the purpose of my observations was to search for patterns of reading in the group that could direct my whole-class teaching.

Pattern 1: Retelling as Recitation

Many students were able to pack the story into their heads as they read. That is, when asked to retell, they never once looked back at the text and yet were able to accurately recount what happened in the story. At first, I did not think of this as particularly important. After all, reading is not a memory test. But as I watched others struggle with retelling, I realized that the ability to tell the story from memory revealed a kind of engagement with the text that would allow for greater connections and deeper, more insightful interpretations later.

Those who struggled with retelling did so in a small handful of ways. Some had to keep looking back to remind themselves what had happened each step of the way. These readers were mostly able to take their eyes off the page once their memory had returned. Still other readers never took their eyes off the page and, instead of retelling the story, would almost recite the text. That is, as they were "retelling," they would look at the page and use most of the words found there. It sounded something like the record sheet below:

Actual Text	Retelling That Sounds Like Recition

The night before last I dreamed that Cynthia Slater asked my opinion of *The Catcher in the Rye*.
    Last night I dreamed I told Lauren Lake what I thought of John Lennon's music, Picasso's art and Soviet-American relations.
    It's getting worse.
    I'm tired of putting my head under the cold-water faucet.
    Early this morning my father came into my room and said, "John, are you getting serious with Eleanor Rossi?" (93)
	So the night before last he dreamed that Cynthia asked his opinion of *Catcher in the Rye*. Last night he dreamed he told Lauren about John Lennon's music, Picasso's art, and Soviet-American relations. He's tired of putting his head under the cold-water faucet. Then early in the morning his father came into his room and asked, "Are you getting serious with Eleanor?"

My sense was that this kind of reading revealed something about the way kids were building the world of the text in their minds and holding onto the story as they read. I wondered about the pictures these readers made in their heads. Instead of making a movie that evolved as the story unfolded, my guess was that these readers were seeing a set of tiny details that passed by individually or, maybe they were seeing nothing at all.

Pattern 2: Problems with Accumulating the Story

Kids who retold the story well also did so in the general order that the story unfolded. They recognized that the parts of the story had something to do with one another and that in building the world of the text, they needed to make connections between the parts. Other kids did not accumulate the story in this way. They acted as if the parts of the story had nothing to do with one another.

For example, some kids acted as if the writer kept changing subjects. While these readers did put the story into a correct sequence, they did not seem to connect the parts and show how they built on one another to create a whole text. In this kind of reading, they might say:

> First they're talking about dreams he has, then his dad talks to him about a girl he likes, then he goes to school with another girl, then he goes to the bathroom to smoke . . .

Other kids kind of "poked" at the parts of the text. They'd list things that had happened but in no particular order. In this kind of reading, they might say:

> He's tired of putting cold water on his head and he had a dream he told Lauren about the music and art, and his dad asked him if he was serious about Eleanor.

Other kids revealed a failure to accumulate the story by simply skipping parts. They acted as if and sometimes even said that some parts were un-important, as if the writer were simply wasting words on the page. For example, many readers skipped the part when John goes down to breakfast after his father leaves his room. In this passage, the text takes us into John's thinking as he tries to imagine the last time his parents shared their thoughts.

> I don't think they've exchanged an idea in years.
> To tell you the truth, I can't imagine them exchanging ideas, ever, though I know they did. She has a collection of letters he wrote to her on every subject from Shakespeare to Bach, and he treasures this little essay she wrote for him when they were engaged, on her feelings about French drama.
> All I've ever seen them do is hug and kiss. Maybe they wait until I'm asleep to get into their discussions. Who knows? (94)

Some readers paid attention to this part. I am not suggesting that readers need to pay equal, intense attention to every detail as they read, but I do think they should consider the possibility that hiding in the details might be ideas they've never thought of before. This is not to say that every detail matters, but only that kids should position themselves to consider details before dismissing them. Kids who paid attention to this part of the story used it first to confirm and then to extend notions they were developing about how this story was different from others about teens and puberty and love. Then they used it to think about how kids perceive their parents.

Pattern 3: A Failure to Question Inconsistencies and Ironies

This story turns conventional ideas on their heads. Most kids took pause at details that seemed unconventional to them. What happened after the pauses created a distinction in my mind between different kinds of readers. Some kids noticed something different about the text and simply responded by saying that it was weird. In this kind of reading, they might say:

> Wait, the teacher kisses the student? Are they allowed to do that? That's weird.

Other kids asked smart questions to examine these parts and try to make greater sense of them. "Wait," they said, "why are there heads drawn on the bathroom walls and why do the parents get upset about Thoughts class?" Kids who were asking these kinds of questions were able to use big understandings they had about the world to develop compelling interpretations of the story. They recognized not only that the story was about growing up and schooling and the way kids and parents perceive each other but also that there was a twist in the story. They recognized that unlike in our own society, where physical affection is private and intellectual exploration public, in this society the two were reversed, and they used that understanding to consider the consequences of a world like that and to think about what the text might want us to comprehend about our world.

Pattern 4: Changing the Story to Fit Preconceived Categories

Many kids in the class tried to apply familiar concepts to the text as a way to place it in a certain category. Sometimes kids would bring their understandings of the genre to their meaning making. These kids recognized the text as containing dystopian elements and used their knowledge of these elements to make sense of the text.

Other kids saw a pattern or idea in the text that was familiar to them in the world and used it to help explain their thinking. This was a smart way to make sense of the text. Some kids, however, used these categories as ends to their thinking. "This is a growing-up story," they'd say, or "This is a love story." When kids used this kind of recognition as the beginning of their thinking, it was helpful in developing nuanced interpretations of the text. When kids saw the category as an end, it stifled them and led them to think that every story that fit into the category was the same. They didn't try to uncover any complexity or uniqueness. In this kind of reading, they might say:

> Oh, this is a story about teenagers and the stuff they go through. It's about teens and love. John likes all these girls, but his dad doesn't want him to rush into anything.

Students who read this way missed markers that could have helped them see that this text was trying to position them to think differently about the story world and the real world. For example:

- "Stick to lovemaking," [John's dad said to him].
- On the bathroom wall there are heads drawn with kids' initials inside.
- The bathroom wall graffiti says, "Josephine Merrill is a brain! I'd love to know her opinions!"

Pattern 5: Seeing Books as an End Rather Than a Beginning

The last pattern I saw clearly indicated a reading strength as well as a weakness because most kids were able to bring understandings that they had about the world to this text. The fact that they were able to place the text in a category of "stories like that" showed that they had some interpretive skill. The trouble was that they used these categorical ideas to tie the story up neatly. They used them as answers to the story, as ways to end thinking as opposed to ways to open up thinking and connect the story to other texts and their own lives.

The kids seemed to read as if the story didn't matter, as if it didn't contain anything that could provoke them or make them think or affect them in any way. Few kids, when asked to comment on what they thought the text was really all about, had anything to say other than, "I agree. Parents and kids are like that." I knew that I needed not only to teach the kids strategies that would help them make sense of the texts they were reading but also to encourage them to consider that texts had something to offer them, that they could come to care about what they were reading.

Making a Plan from the Assessment

With all of this in mind, and with a clear vision of my belief in helping kids use reading to explore concerns in their lives, I had to make a decision about what direction my teaching would take for the year. I looked through my research to figure out what needed to come early in the year and what I could put off until later. I had noticed that overall, kids seemed so distant from their reading. Because of this and because I knew that developing a stronger relationship to books was fundamental to seeing reading as a way to build a world, I decided to begin with a unit of study on bringing reading closer. The unit would help kids see themselves in books and use that connection to begin to care about what they were reading. Later, after many more kids saw what was possible through reading, I would take up what I had noticed about their difficulties with reading carefully and thoughtfully.

Step Back and Reflect

This early assessment not only directed my whole-class teaching for the year but also set the stage for a way of being as a teacher. The process of creating a way to see what my kids were doing as readers and then trying to name patterns of strength and struggle for the purpose of finding teaching points was incredibly useful and one I would use over and over again throughout the year.

In the past, I often had trouble creating minilessons. I'd embark on a unit of study and then struggle with what to teach. Often when I pulled alongside a student for a conference, whatever she was doing felt pretty good to me, so I'd just compliment her and move on. If things were going poorly in my room, I'd blame the workshop format.

I have since learned that when trouble shows its face in my room, I'm lucky. You see, I now view trouble as possibility. I see it as an opportunity to teach, as the content of my lessons. In fact, now I not only hope for trouble but search for it. I constantly try to problematize my kids' work so that I can think about things to teach them. Sometimes it feels like I am complaining about them a lot or focusing only on what they cannot do. But while I try to be sensitive to looking for strengths to build on, I am not afraid to name struggles. It's there that I find my best cues for teaching.

Think About Your Classroom

◆ Create some tools that will allow you to gather general information about your kids' experiences as readers. Your goal is to find out what reading has been like for them. In what ways have they felt successful? In what ways have they struggled? If you have developed some theories or concerns about the kids right from the start, you might want to develop a questionnaire that asks really tough questions that will immediately address those concerns.

◆ Find a short text that will help you see what it looks like when your kids are reading. (Pick one that is short enough so that students have time to read it and then meet with you in one period.) You probably want to find a text in which the kids will be able to read all the words but will have difficulties understanding the message. You want a text that has multiple layers of meaning so that you can see multiple levels of reading. Often a story that is set either far away or long ago, such as historical fiction, science fiction, or foreign fiction, provides these layers. It should allow the kids to apply what they know and understand about the world to make sense of this situation but also allow them to move beyond their experience and see some differences. The list of short text collections I've provided in the back of this book might be a place to start.

◆ Create a form to record your observations from the kids' reading. Although a checklist is often appealing, you probably want to avoid a checklist because the purpose of your research is to discover and describe what your kids are doing, not just confirm what you already think. A simple chart that will allow you to record their retellings and describe what you notice about the ideas they develop from the story should suffice.

◆ Look for patterns in their reading. Spend time reading over your notes and looking for the ways in which the kids did or did not make sense of the text. What did they do to make sense? What didn't they understand? What got in their way?

◆ Turn your discoveries into curriculum. Try to sort and categorize the ideas you found into units of study. Lay these categories next to your goals for the year and use them shape the units. That is, include them as subtopics inside the units and develop minilessons out of them. Don't try to teach about everything you've noticed in September. Decide what you need to teach first and hold off on the rest.

....

CHAPTER 4

Making Reading Matter
Strengthening Our Relationships to Books

Kids are so easily influenced by each other. They tend to wear the same clothing, and listen to the same music. When some new trend or interest hits the school, it spreads like wildfire.

By mid-September, when I decided to take up the issue of learning how to let books affect us personally as my first major unit of study, I realized I could bank on this group power. I knew that helping kids see that reading could matter in their lives would be challenging, especially with kids for whom reading had always been a struggle and those who would never choose to spend their time reading. Maybe, however, if I could create some energy around reading in the large group, I could get more and more kids to buy in.

The workshop structures that best use the group to explore an idea are the read-aloud and the literature discussion. During these activities, kids have the opportunity to work as a large group to share their thinking and develop new ideas. Typically, I gather the kids in the meeting area and read aloud from a short text. While they listen, they think about what's worth discussing in the book. They jot those ideas down in their literacy notebooks and when I finish reading, they turn to the person next to them to get their voices going and share their initial thinking. Then the group conversation begins with a couple of students offering some possible topics. The talk passes from student to student much in the same way dinner conversation passes. They know it's their turn to talk because no one else is talking. In this way, the kids, and not I, control the topic of the conversation and the turn taking. I talk only if there's a problem or to reflect on the quality of the talk.

Because the conversation is controlled by the kids, it's an opportunity for them to really work on listening to each other and trying to come under the influence of each other's words. It's the time of the week when we understand that learning does not happen in isolation and that we can grow simply by interacting with others.

Research into Book Discussions

Like most aspects of reading workshop, I knew I couldn't make any assumptions about what kids could do during a book discussion. I needed to watch. I trusted that the way the kids talked about the books would reveal some things about their attitudes. My goal was to uncover what the kids knew about how to talk well about books and what prevented them from being able to connect to books meaningfully. I knew that I could then turn those discoveries into minilessons that could possibly reshape their relationship to books.

To prepare for these first conversations, I developed a list of qualities of good discussion that I would be looking for. I wrote this list on the top of a notepad on which I would jot down what I noticed during the conversations. I wanted to see whether or not the kids would do the following:

◆ Display good turn-taking behaviors. I wanted to see if the kids would pay attention not only when they wanted to say something but also when their classmates did. I knew that turn taking is needed to grow ideas together.

◆ Try to connect what they had read and talked about with things that mattered to them. I knew that readers who saw books as potential tools to examine the world tried to make connections between a text and the world they know, and often those connections are topics of discussion for them. I wanted to see whether the kids would notice this.

◆ Use themselves or people they knew as examples to stretch their ideas about the story. If the kids did this, it would mean that they saw the text as having to do with them and that they could think between the details of the text and the details of their own lives.

◆ React emotionally. I wondered whether anyone would get mad or excited. Emotion can reveal investment. While it's not necessarily true that a lack of outward emotion reveals a lack of investment, when kids do show their emotions, we have a window into their thinking. When we let books make us mad or sad or excited, we are engaging personally with them.

◆ Try to question some of the underlying assumptions in the text. Too often kids respond to texts either as authorities or as made-up tales in which anything goes. Neither of these beliefs helps kids develop a critical eye toward their texts or allows them to use texts in ways that develop imaginations.

I focused on these qualities because they got at ideas foundational to our current work and our ability to grow together throughout the year. Additionally, keeping this list in front of me helped me focus my attention and avoid getting involved in the conversation. To further support my research, I positioned myself outside the group and told the kids to begin. During the first couple of discussions, I just listened and took notes.

My first read-aloud was Richard Peck's "Priscilla and the Wimps" (1985). "Priscilla and the Wimps" is a story of school and bullying and gangs and outcasts and retribution. The story is narrated by Melvin, who tells of Monk Klutter and his gang, Klutter's Kobras, who run the school. They steal lunch money and sell bathroom passes and are generally feared in school—except by Priscilla, Melvin's best friend, who seems to have never heard of the Kobras. One day, however, Priscilla walks into a scene in which one of the Kobras is picking on Melvin. This leads to an altercation with Monk that ends with him being stuck in a locker for what turns out to be two weeks—the result of a sudden snowstorm that closes school.

I chose this story first because it is very short—only four pages in length. This was important because I wanted to complete the whole process of reading aloud and discussing in one session. Also I knew that even good conversations often begin with participants batting around ideas in search of a worthy topic, so a short work would allow a lot of time to talk and, I hoped, show me all that the kids could do.

I also chose "Priscilla and the Wimps" because it provides great opportunities for kids to show what they think about when they read. I just knew that some kids would listen and feel validated by the way in which Priscilla is both oblivious to Monk and his gang and also willing to fight him. Other kids, I suspected, would question the believability of the story, arguing that school just doesn't go that way. Picking a story that could possibly provoke the kids into an active discussion, even an argument, would show how they let the ideas in stories affect them.

I gathered the kids in the meeting area, told them to have their notebooks in front of them so they could record their thinking, and then asked them to listen to the story carefully so that they would be able to discuss it afterward. I wanted to position the kids as listeners—to remind them that their job was to focus on the reading and to prepare themselves for the discussion.

After the reading I explained to the kids that now they were supposed to talk. I told them that they needn't raise their hands because I wasn't going to call on people. They'd know it was their turn to talk when no one else was talking. The topic and direction of discussion were up to them. I trusted that they would have something to say and that they could conduct a discussion themselves.

Retelling What Happened in the Story

What was most striking in this early conversation, which also ended up recurring throughout many discussions, was the way some kids talked about what happened in the story.

Byron spoke first. "She shoved him in the locker and he was stuck there for two weeks."

There was a long pause and then Robert spoke. "Yeah, he was picking on Melvin and she just grabbed him by the neck and threw him in the locker."

A few giggles. And then silence. And then Kim. "They'd make the kids give them their lunch money."

It was as if they were simply retelling parts of the story, just sharing out loud what happened. They weren't really discussing anything. There wasn't even an order to the way they retold. It was as if they did not imagine they could think about what happened in the story and develop ideas about it.

This was very surprising to me. I had expected that perhaps the talk would be somewhat distant from the kids, but I didn't expect that they would mostly retell without even commenting at all. Why was this? Was it that they simply saw themselves as doing schoolwork and in school the teacher wants you to show that you know what happened in the story? Was it that they had some thoughts about the story but didn't know how to talk about them? Or did they simply not connect? My sense was that the answer was somewhere in the middle. I knew I needed to provide opportunities for them to engage in many more book discussions so I could search for patterns in their work.

Finding Quick Answers

There were, of course, some kids who were able to develop some thinking about the story. But even for the most perceptive kids, the thinking often felt small or—more often—was left small. For example, after a bit of retelling around the text, Amanda said, "Why do you think Priscilla didn't know Monk?"

"The school is probably big, so not everyone knows everyone," Katie responded.

"And she keeps to herself. She's a loner type," Tim replied.

And then Sonia, changing the subject, asked, "Where were the teachers? Why didn't they do anything about the Kobras?"

"Because teachers don't ever do anything."

And then there was another long pause. After a while a new conversation began. I had expected more kids to respond to the issue of Monk's power. I had expected them to explore the implications of what was raised in the group. I had hoped that someone would wonder how it could be that Priscilla didn't really know Monk if he was so powerful in school or how

Monk even got all that power. I had hoped someone would say whether the story represented his or her school experience and what new meaning he or she could make of that.

All of these early comments are, however, typical of the way even the most successful conversations start. Often conversations begin with people poking around the text as they search for and try out little ideas. But the problem here was that, unlike most successful conversations, this one never went anywhere. There was never a moment when the group got excited about one thing and stayed with it long enough to create new thinking. It appeared that the conversation had caused no one to think about things in new ways, ways that mattered to him or her. It felt as if the kids simply checked this text off a list of schoolwork they had completed.

While I had hoped that the kids would listen to the text in a way that would let them develop a thought or opinion and then use the conversation to develop that idea, instead I found the beginning of my whole-class teaching. I now realized that I could begin my next set of minilessons by teaching the kids how to find something thoughtful to say. I could develop lessons that would teach them what it sounded like to raise questions about texts and to explore those questions deeply.

Read-Aloud Lessons That Helped

Bringing Us Closer to the Story

In these early conversations the kids kept the stories far away from themselves: That is, they didn't make any personal connections with their reading. There was always the feeling that these were made-up people in made-up situations. No one ever responded to "Priscilla and the Wimps" by saying anything like, "I know people who bully and I can't stand it," or "I have friends who are so different from me and people often wonder how we can be friends." It was as if they hadn't yet imagined they could say something like this.

I decided that my first lessons to accompany the read-aloud sessions would be geared to teaching them to see these personal connections. I continued using "Priscilla and the Wimps." We gathered in the meeting area as we did every time we had a read-aloud and I began my lesson.

"I know that most of you have had the experience of reading a book and realizing that something in the story reminded you of something in your own lives. Today I want to show you how those personal connections can help you in literature discussion. They can be a way to stretch out your ideas and, in turn, a way to use the text to think about your own lives. Let's take a look at part of a transcript of our last conversation about 'Priscilla and the Wimps.'" I put the transcript up on the overhead.

First Conversation About "Priscilla and the Wimps"

Amanda: Why do you think Priscilla didn't know Monk?

Katie: The school is probably big, so not everyone knows everyone.

Tim: And she keeps to herself. She's a loner type.

Sonia: Where were the teachers?

"Notice how in the original discussion, Sonia switched the topic. Today, I want to show you how you can use your personal connections to explore an idea more deeply and to imagine ways to use the story to help you think about your own life. Let's look at a revised version of the conversation, one that uses personal connections. As I read through it, think about how the personal connection helps bring the story closer to the group and improves the conversation."

Revised Conversation About "Priscilla and the Wimps"

Amanda: Why do you think Priscilla didn't know Monk?

Katie: The school is probably big, so not everyone knows everyone.

Tim: And she keeps to herself. She's a loner type.

Student A: I can understand how Monk had never heard of Priscilla. We go to a small school and there are people who are invisible here.

Student B: Yeah, there are probably kids here that I don't know. They're not my friends and they don't stand out in any way. Like, everyone knows the popular kids and everyone knows the kids who kind of stand out. We all know Beth because she's really smart and always argues with everyone. And we know Stuart because he gets in trouble all the time, but sometimes I walk down the hall and see people I don't know at all.

Student A: I think it's more likely that the unpopular kids are invisible. I mean, I'm not really that popular and sometimes I'm sort of ignored. I was sitting at the lunch table waiting for a friend the other day and a group of kids sat down at the table and totally ignored me. They didn't even bother to ask whether anyone was sitting there. They just assumed it was open for them. I can imagine that Monk is that way with Priscilla. Priscilla must not be popular.

When I finished reading through the revised transcript, I asked the kids to turn to the person next to them and share what they noticed. Then I re-read "Priscilla and the Wimps" and encouraged the kids to try to focus on personal connections that they could use in our next conversation.

During the conversation that followed, the kids took up the same question I had shown in the transcript. How was it that Priscilla didn't know Monk? And while the ideas they explored didn't stray far from those I presented in the example, the opportunity to try using personal connections to linger on an idea paid off in later talks.

Learning to Connect to Each Other's Ideas

Listening to these conversations, I also realized that as the kids kept themselves distant from the texts, they also kept themselves distant from each other. They struggled to listen hard to what others were saying and had difficulty responding in ways that opened up more thinking. Often the kids responded to each other in ways that were dismissive or that closed down new opportunities for thinking.

At first I thought this was a language issue. Maybe I needed to teach the kids that there was language they could use to help them stay on a topic for a while. To linger on an idea, students can use phrases like

- ◆ I agree/disagree with . . .
- ◆ I want to add on . . .
- ◆ It makes me think . . .
- ◆ I wonder whether . . .
- ◆ So what you're saying is . . .

I began to teach lessons that showed kids how to use this language. These lessons often took the form of fishbowl discussions in which I was a member of the discussion group. I'd gather a small group of kids together with me in the middle of the meeting area to discuss a short story. The rest of the kids would gather around us to research what we were doing. In these lessons, I used a strategy I had learned from a good teacher friend of mine, Kathy Collins, who taught first grade in Brooklyn for a number of years. I told the kids that I was going to be Donna, an eighth grader, discussing the story with my classmates. I then asked the larger group to watch the way I used language to connect my ideas to others' thoughts.

These lessons took hold quickly and I began hearing kids use the phrases in their talk. This created an immediate improvement in the quality of the conversations, and I realized how important it is to model for kids simple moves they can make in conversation. So often we think kids don't have the language to participate in class conversations thoughtfully. But none of the phrases I taught the kids was new to them. What was new was naming them as phrases they could always use and showing them how to apply these phrases to a literature discussion for the purpose of extending their thinking.

Despite the power of these early lessons, however, sometimes the conversations still felt small. Sometimes, even though they had the language to open up conversations, some kids used it in ways that closed them down. They would say things like, "I agree with everything that's been said and . . . ," and then go on to say something totally disconnected to what was being discussed. The language became just another thing to do, not really a tool to support deeper thinking.

I knew then that I would need to teach some harder concepts. I had to help the kids understand that the real power in conversation is in the mind of the listener. The words of the speaker matter less than the way you listen. I wanted kids to understand that the goal was not to find answers to the ideas that were raised, but to introduce more interesting questions. I wanted them to see literature discussion as a performative act in which they could explore problems rather than avoid them and imagine alternative ways of thinking rather than dismiss them (Blau 2003).

I also knew, however, that it was still fairly early in the year. I knew that later curriculum on learning how to interpret texts might be a better time to explore these issues, so I decided to take on the issue of simply learning more about how to have a discussion for now. This was, I decided, the best way to help kids strengthen their relationships to books.

Having a Discussion Versus Making a Statement

Book talk is more than a share session. Even though the kids started to use language that was meant to help them connect their ideas, they often commented on things they had already been thinking instead of sharing new thoughts in response to their peers' ideas. Additionally, the conversations felt flat. I often found myself thinking, "So what?" And the longer the conversation, the fewer the kids who talked. It was as if many of us were asking, "Who cares?"

I began by telling the kids that in a book talk their job was to find a topic and then talk in a way that invited discussion rather than simply share a comment. "I've noticed that someone says something and then lots of us just nod our heads. Then, after a bit, someone says something else—maybe it's connected or maybe not. But there's no real sense of discussion. Early in a conversation we might just share our comments, but this is for the purpose of finding something to discuss. To do this, you need to think more about the way you say things. You have to *invite* each other into the conversation. You have to make each other want to care, want to talk back.

"The easiest way to do that is to end your comment with a question. When you question, you're asking someone to answer. But you can also make your comment sound more like wondering with particular words. For example, if you begin by saying, 'It seems to me . . . ,' or 'I'm wondering whether . . . ,' you invite others to join in on your thinking."

I next announced that I was going to read aloud Jean Davies Okimoto's "Moonbeam Dawson and the Killer Bear" (1989). It's the story of a boy, Moonbeam, who lives and works at a fishing lodge. Moonbeam finds himself caught in a lie about having experience hunting bears just to get himself a date with Michelle, who is visiting the lodge for the weekend.

When I was finished reading, I encouraged the kids to invite more discussion by trying out the language I had mentioned earlier. Alexandra started the discussion. "Moonbeam seems to me to be like a lot of boys," she began. "He'll do anything to impress girls, even lie."

"Yeah, they always do that," Kathy responded.

Debbie then added, "I wonder why. Why do you think boys lie to impress girls?"

"I don't think it's just boys. I think girls do it too," Robert offered. "I know lots of girls who say things that aren't true to get a guy to pay attention to them."

The conversation continued, going back and forth as the kids tried to prove whether or not boys were the only liars. And even though the discussion seemed to jump up and down in place, in a "yes they do, no they don't" rhythm, it was encouraging to watch them discuss something.

Bringing Independent Reading Closer

At the same time that I was helping kids see themselves in books through read-alouds, I took on the same task with independent reading. This transfer of understandings to independent reading from read-alouds was important because, after all, everything I taught was ultimately meant to affect the way kids read independently, outside of school.

But I had concerns. I had watched kids make and then share personal connections for years. The connections often led to ineffective reading and ineffective talk. I knew that often when we teach kids to make personal connections, they end up poking around the book, letting it remind them of this and that in their lives. "The kid in the article has a cell phone; so do I." "The girl in the story fights with her little sister; so do I." Very often, these connections lead to great stories about times we've used our cell phones or moments of sibling rivalry, but they often leave the text behind and don't generate new thinking about the topics we're discussing. For years when I heard kids talking in this way I felt so uncomfortable. It sounded as if they were off task and I would try to get them back to the text. But I also noticed that when the kids were talking only about what happened in the text, their ideas were limited. To grow those ideas, perhaps we needed to be willing to bring more of our outside lives to the text.

Learning to Ask "So What?"

Because I wasn't sure how to get the kids to use their personal connections more thoughtfully, I took on a little research with them. I started by asking them to notice when in their reading they were connecting personally to the stories and to mark those passages with sticky notes. Pretty quickly the kids' books started filling up with notes. Malik marked the place in Walter Dean Myers' "Christmas Story" (2000) where the character of Mother Fletcher reminded him of a lady on his block. Sonia marked the place in Martha Brooks' "Where Has All the Romance Gone?" (1994b) where Lindsey's grandparents reminded her of her own. We did this for a few days and then gathered in the meeting area for a minilesson designed to help us think about how to make more of our connections.

"We've been focusing these last couple of days on noticing our personal connections. And in some ways, none of this is new. You've shared personal connections almost as long as you've been reading. But today I want to ask you a big question: *So what?* Why do these connections matter?"

Isaac, my class philosopher, started our talk. "Sometimes, when I make a personal connection," he began, "I stop and think more about it and maybe when I do that I understand the story more. Maybe I understand how the character is feeling or why [he's] doing what [he's] doing and it helps me understand more about [him]."

Then Joclyn added, "Yeah, and sometimes it helps me think about myself more, too. Like when I was reading *Crusader,* by Edward Bloor [1999], I got to thinking about how the kids who play the racist video games in the book were kind of like this kid Tony that some of us know. He is so racist and when I was reading the book, I was thinking about how the main character was struggling with trying to stand up to all of this and how I'm also struggling with how to stand up to Tony. I mean, he says the scariest things, but for some reason I just let it happen. I never say anything back.

It's not exactly the same as *Crusader*, but it just got me thinking that about myself."

I was struck by how quickly and easily the kids were able to talk about the role of personal connections in their reading. It felt so different from the book discussions kids were having. As I listened, I noticed something important—something that made me shift the way I felt and taught about the personal connections the kids were making. I realized that if I let the kids talk more about the connections, without worrying that they were no longer talking about the books, they would move beyond just ignoring the connection or simply naming it and start making meaning from it. Therefore, I decided that instead of being afraid to let kids talk about things they were reminded of when they read, I'd let them talk long and expect them to try to articulate their new understandings about their books and their lives.

What's the That?

As we shared our stories, another type of connection emerged. This happened more often when we connected to books on an emotional level. It's when we found ourselves saying, "I've felt like that before. I know how that goes." When this happened I taught the kids to ask, "What's the *that*? What's the *that* you felt when Jeannie, after being pushed into the boys' bathroom in Frances Lantz's story 'Standing on the Roof Naked' [2003], couldn't even thank the boy who came to her rescue? What's the *that* you felt when you were reading Ray Bradbury's *Dandelion Wine* [1946] and Doug's dad didn't understand why Doug so desperately needed a new pair of sneakers?" Asking ourselves "What's the *that*?" forces us to make more of our connections. It asks us to generalize between the story and ourselves and therefore find new ways to think about our lives. It helps us imagine new ways to respond to our parents, our siblings, and our peers.

It wasn't easy getting the kids to find the words to answer "What's the *that*?" They'd often shrug their shoulders and say, "I don't know how to explain it." They'd just give up. But I knew I needed to stick with it. So I began to ask the kids to slow down their minds, to be patient. Finding words takes time. The silence that surrounds kids as they search their minds for words to explain their ideas often feels deafening. It's incredibly tempting to fill that void with questions that will lead them through some thinking. I have learned, however, that I need to be patient, too. I need to allow them the time to trust that I really do want *them* to find the words to explain what they're connecting to.

I also need to be patient enough to find ways to teach them how to think about their ideas as opposed to leading them to my thinking. Sometimes I have found that if I think aloud a couple of possible explanations for their ideas, the model provides enough to get them going and teaches them the kinds of words they might use themselves next time.

Step Back and Reflect

In years past, I've always started my reading workshop with units of study that focused kids' attention on choosing books that were right for them and learning to read for understanding. I wanted the kids to have in their hands books they could read and wanted to read. I wanted to teach them right from the start that books are supposed to make sense and that strong readers have strategies for ensuring that they do so. And every year, as the months passed, I struggled as more and more kids disregarded the strategies and just skipped past their confusions.

Then, one afternoon, during a lunchtime discussion with a group of district staff developers, someone raised the question of payoff. What payoff is there for kids to do the work of understanding their reading? I've carried that question with me ever since. And this year when my early assessment revealed a kind of slurry, disconnected reading, I decided to turn that question from one that I simply carried in my mind into one that drove early curriculum. I decided to help kids see the payoff in reading, that reading can raise issues of concern for us and help us think through those concerns. I decided to show my kids a new way of thinking about reading, one that repositioned them to care more about the potential that reading offered instead of simply completing, or looking like they were completing, their schoolwork.

Think About Your Classroom

◆ Begin to help your kids see that they can have a strong relationship to books through read-alouds and literature discussions. That is, take plenty of time early in the year to read aloud and teach kids how to connect to texts.

◆ Find texts that will provide kids with easy opportunities to connect with their reading right from the start. When the connections are not too difficult to make, you'll be able to see how far your kids can go with their thinking.

◆ Begin read-aloud work by finding out what kids understand about how to use their discussions to explore ideas they care about. Always start by doing research. Don't assume you know what the kids need to learn about book talk. Step out of the discussion so you can see what they can do on their own.

◆ After a few research sessions, gather up your notes and reread them. Jot down everything you notice about their talk. What did they talk about? How did they take turns talking? Did they try to connect with what they read? Did they use themselves or people they knew as examples to stretch their ideas? Did they react emotionally to the text? Search for patterns related to these questions. Figure out what to teach now and what to save for later by matching up your research to your yearlong goals. Don't be afraid to save things for later.

◆ Turn your ideas into minilessons. These lessons can take the form of fishbowls, in which a small group of students joins you in front of the group to demonstrate how to use a talk strategy in a discussion. You might also type up a short transcript of a conversation to serve as an example of a strategy you want to teach.

◆ Make sure kids understand that making a personal connection is about more than naming the ways we are like or not like the characters in the books we are reading. Making a personal connection is about exploring what these attributes say about us as people. It also means connecting to the text on an emotional level and examining those emotions.

◆ After you work on your goals for a while in read-alouds and discussions, bring the same goals into your minilessons and conferences when students are reading independently.

....

CHAPTER 5

Getting It
Learning to Attend to More of the Text

B
y mid-October the class started to change. Kids began to talk *to* each other as opposed to *at* each other. Reading conferences revealed a slight increase in thinking as the kids read. I even heard a few hall-way conversations involving books. Most often, they were in the form of rec-ommendations, but the reasons for suggesting the book usually revealed some kind of connection the reader had discovered in the book.

And while I was feeling somewhat excited about the reading commu-nity we were building, I was also feeling some tension. Quite a number of reading conferences revealed a kind of "getting what I need" reading. The kids were reading to make connections, were learning to determine impor-tance for themselves, but this often meant they disregarded whole chunks of the texts they were reading. They were skipping through the stories— almost understanding them but often not quite.

To read well is to acknowledge the relationship between the text and the reader. Our reading is directed not only by our responses to the text but also by the text itself. Louise Rosenblatt (1978) explains that reading requires an openness through which the reader brings his or her own context to cre-ate meaning, but it also requires an attention to the exact words of the text. Rosenblatt describes the text as providing a blueprint that guides and helps us check our meaning making.

I had chosen to start with the unit on trying to develop a stronger rela-tionship with reading so that the kids would feel a greater desire to work at understanding their books. Yet, the opportunity would be lost if the kids felt like they could read well *only* by thinking about how parts of the books connected to their own lives. Therefore I decided I needed to focus some quick, clear attention on helping kids attend to a greater portion of the texts they were reading.

So I began a new unit of study, one that would center on learning how to build the world of the whole text as you read it. In this unit, I wanted kids to understand the following:

- ◆ Building the world of the text means seeing and hearing the text as you read. To support our growing ability to do this, we can try to say the text aloud in our minds in a way that makes it make sense.
- ◆ Sometimes when we read, we lose understanding. When this happens, we can temporarily interrupt our reading to retell.
- ◆ Good readers try to pack some of the details of the story into my mind. We try to hold onto characters' names and where the story is taking place so that we can get a fuller picture of the text and begin to develop some thinking.
- ◆ Good readers recognize that the parts of the text go together to build a whole and always try to keep in mind how each part connects to what came before.

And to ensure that the kids would feel the need to try the strategies I was planning to introduce to them, I asked them to pick books they thought might require them to do some work—books on the edge of their reading ability. The kids needed "optimal books," books that would force them to use explicit reading strategies in order to comprehend (Fielding and Pearson 1994). If they felt they were reading books that were a little challenging, they would be more willing to reach for the strategies.

Saying Fiction with Words That Clarify Meaning

As the kids began choosing optimal books, I began my teaching. For each of these lessons, I put a short text up on the overhead and thought aloud for the kids, sharing with them what was going through my mind as I read the text to myself. This process of talking aloud about how I made sense of the text provided the kids with a model of thinking I wanted them to take on as their own (Wilhelm 2001). First I wanted to show the kids that as I read, I try to say the text aloud in my mind in a way that makes it make sense.

I began once again with Richard Peck's "Priscilla and the Wimps" (1985). I asked them to notice what I was doing while I read so they'd be able to describe it at the end of the demonstration. I did not read the text aloud to the kids. Instead I read it in my head and while I was doing so, I tried to say the text to myself (see below). That is, I tried to reword it so that it made sense to me.

After repeated demonstrations like this over the next few days, I sent kids off to read independently. As I sent them off, I told them that I expected them to try to read in a way that would make the texts clear to them. I told them that some of them might want to talk out loud while others would

Actual Text (read silently)	Saying the Text So That It Makes Sense
Listen, there was a time when you couldn't even go to the rest room around this school without a pass. And I'm not talking about those little pink tickets made out by some teacher. I'm talking about a pass that could cost anywhere up to a buck, sold by Monk Klutter.	It used to be that you couldn't even go to the bathroom without a pass sold to you by Monk Klutter, some kid in school.
Not that Mighty Monk ever touched money, not in public. The gang he ran, which ran the school for him, was his collection agency. They were Klutter's Kobras, a name spelled out in nailheads on six well-known black plastic windbreakers.	Monk didn't collect the money. No, you paid one of the Klutter's Kobras, the guys in his gang who ran the school for him. You could recognize them by the black jackets they wore with the gang name on the back.

probably just say their version of the text in their heads. I spent the independent reading time traveling from student to student, conferring around this work and looking for patterns of difficulty. These patterns became future minilessons. I taught kids how to apply this strategy across genres (see the following section) as well as what to do when the text became confusing or there were too many characters or time shifts to hold onto.

Saying Nonfiction in Ways That Make It Understandable

In past years, my reading workshops have been fiction heavy. This year, right from the start, I pushed nonfiction reading, especially magazine and newspaper reading, two genres that help kids engage with current issues and events and the two probably most often read by adults. Because of this, by the time we reached this unit of study, kids were reading *Upfront, Choices, Muse*, and a number of other magazines I had subscriptions to in the classroom. As I conferred with the students, I realized that their struggles with making the text come alive in their minds were present with nonfiction as well as fiction. The kids had trouble with putting the text together in ways that helped them understand how the parts connected. They struggled to determine importance in the details for themselves. That is, they didn't distinguish between details that were illustrative of larger ideas and details that might be worth holding onto in their minds.

It made sense then, to spend some time showing the kids how to apply the same strategy of saying the text in their minds to an article or essay. For one particular lesson, I chose an article from *Nutrition Action Newsletter*, a newsletter published by the Center for Science in the Public Interest. This particular article, "What a Pizza Delivers" (Jones et al. 2002), explored the debate about whether pizza is or is not healthy.

I began by gathering the kids in the meeting area. On the overhead was a copy of the first page of the article. "Over the last couple of days we've been talking about how to read and say the texts in order to make them make sense to us," I told them. "Today, I want to show you how I apply this same strategy to a piece of nonfiction. I have on the overhead an article about eating pizza from *Nutrition Action Newsletter*. I chose it because it's interesting to me. I eat a lot of pizza and I know that the newsletter often teaches me things about food that affect my eating decisions. Just like with the short fiction we've been looking at, I'm going to read the text in my mind and demonstrate for you how I say it aloud in a way that will make it understandable. Watch what I'm doing so that you will be able to try it a little yourself when I'm done." (See below.)

When finished, I turned to the students and asked them to try it a little with the person sitting next to them. While they practiced for about three minutes, just to get the feel of it, I scooted around the group and listened in a bit. I did this only to hold them accountable to trying, not to fix up any problems I saw. That would happen in later lessons and conferences. I then closed the lesson by reminding the kids that they needed to try these strategies in their reading and that I'd talk to them about their work in our conferences.

Actual Text	Saying the Text So That It Makes Sense
If you don't want to cook or eat out, a pizza is often the default. One out of every six restaurants in the U.S. is a pizzeria. Annual sales reach some $30 billion, rivaling only burger joints. And, in 1999, McDonald's purchased a pizza chain called Donato's. What does *that* tell you?	Pizza is what we eat when we want to eat at home but don't want to cook. There are tons of pizza parlors in the United States that make tons of money. Even McDonald's bought a pizza chain.
No one would dispute pizza's popularity, but when it comes to health, you often hear different stories. For many people, pizza is a lousy food, period. On the other hand, some dieticians claim that pizza is nutritious because it has components of each of the four basic food groups.	Everyone agrees pizza is popular, but there's disagreement as to whether it's healthy. Some people say it's not. Others say it is because it covers a lot of the four basic food groups.

Temporarily Interrupting Your Reading to Retell

Sometimes we ask our kids to try strategies that are not always a part of ordinary reading. Readers don't regularly interrupt their reading to retell what they have just read. Think about it. When you're reading a book that is just right for you, one that you understand with ease, your mind is working to make sense as your eyes move down the page. You picture the text and hear it as you are reading, not chunk by chunk. For this reason, the first thing I taught the kids was to practice saying the text aloud as they were reading, not to read a long chunk, then stop and retell, and then read another long chunk and stop and retell. I wanted them to learn to do the reading and retelling simultaneously.

Sometimes, however, when the text is tricky, when you are struggling a bit to get it or find that you have lost comprehension, it is helpful to stop your reading and retell. Often when kids are confused by a part in the text, they just plow through it and keep going. This happens more often with my stronger readers, those who trust that reading is supposed to make sense. Strong readers trust reading so much, in fact, that when they hit a bump in comprehension, they just keep reading, believing that eventually the story will make sense to them again. But this sometimes causes them to misread and misunderstand their texts. They fill in so much that they actually change the story.

Not all kids just read through their confusions. Instead, many kids tell me that when they are confused, they reread the confusing parts. At first I thought they were just telling me something other teachers had taught them because they thought that's what I wanted to hear. After a bit, however, I realized that they were in fact rereading, but it just wasn't helping them understand. Julie, for example, was reading Gary Paulsen's *Puppies, Dogs and Blue Northers* (1998). She had asked me for a conference because she was confused by a part early in the book when Cookie, Paulsen's dog, is in the snow. I asked her to tell me what strategies she had tried to clear up her confusion and she told me that she just kept rereading the confusing part over and over again, but she still didn't get it. I thought about it for a minute and realized that when I am confused, I don't reread the hard part; I actually go back to the last part I understood and start rereading there. Then I read through the hard part, stop and try to retell the whole thing aloud to myself.

After explaining that strategy to Julie, I got her to try it with me. We went back to the last part of the book she understood and started rereading, she in her head and me in mine. We read to ourselves and when we had gotten through the hard part, we stopped. I then decided to demonstrate the retelling so she could hear what it sounded like to put the parts together and make sense of it all. Then I had her try the retelling herself, about the same part, perhaps even using some of the same words I used, just to get a feel for it.

When we were done, I stepped back and named for Julie the process we had just gone through: Find the last place you understood, reread through the hard part, then stop and try to retell the whole thing. I told her that anytime she got lost in this or any other book, she should try this strategy.

Recognizing that Julie was probably not alone in her struggle to figure out confusing parts in her books and acknowledging the connection between this conference and our unit of study, I decided to turn this conference into a minilesson. I told Julie that I wanted to use our work together as an example for the class and then asked to borrow her copy of the book until the end of the day so that I could make an overhead of the sections we worked on. The next day, I put the overhead up and told the story of the conference, demonstrating the strategy for the whole class in the same way I did for Julie.

This is a move I make again and again in my teaching. I carry in my mind ideas about the unit of study as I confer with the kids, and when I come across work that is a good example of the topic we are exploring, I turn it into a lesson. In this way, the kids see more than just my reading demonstrations as models for their work. They also see that their own work and that of their classmates has potential for larger learning.

Packing the Details in Your Mind

Most units of study have a predictable rhythm to them. After a week or so of practice and conferences, I begin to notice patterns of difficulty and confusion and these become later minilessons. This unit of study revealed a handful of confusions. One in particular that I wanted to deal with was the fact that, just as happened in our reading of "Do You Want My Opinion?," many of the kids were not holding onto details of their stories like the characters' names and the setting. When recounting a text to me or saying it in ways that made it logical, the kids would often say things like "this guy" or "these kids" or "her friend" when talking about the characters. This revealed a clouding of the details that made some kids mix up the characters or become confused about where the characters were at points in the story.

The first lesson I taught focused on character. I began by telling the kids that over the past couple of weeks, as I was conferring with them, I noticed that many of them were ignoring the characters' names. "While it's not always necessary to commit a character's name to memory, it is helpful to try to hold onto their names. This allows you to distinguish between characters more easily, which will help you develop new and interesting thinking as you read." I went on to tell them that I was going to demonstrate how

Actual Text (read silently)	Saying the Text to Make Meaning Using the Characters' Names

"Concentrate! Only one hour before showtime, people," Mr. Walker yells. "You're out of sync, son. Stand still. Don't move." A few people giggle. We know who he's shouting at as he taps his baton on the podium.
 	
    Poor Tommy. His voice wasn't bad, deep bass like mine. But he couldn't move in time to the music. I knew he shouldn't have joined our high school gospel chorus.
	So it's almost showtime and Mr. Walker is yelling at someone who's not on the beat.
	
	    Mr. Walker's yelling at Tommy. He can sing, but he can't move in time.

when I say the text to myself, I try to use the characters' names. Again, I had them watch my demonstration with the purpose of being able to try the strategy, this time with a partner using their own independent reading books. I put on the overhead an excerpt from "A Safe Space," by Joyce Hansen (2000). It's the story of a white boy who attends a predominantly African American school and joins the gospel chorus. I began my think-aloud (see chart at bottom of page 60).

When I finished, I asked the kids to turn to the person next to them and talk for a minute about what I did. And then I sent them off to read independently, reminding them that when they read, they needed to be sure to pack the characters' names into their heads.

Thinking About How the Parts Go Together

I discovered once again during this unit that many kids acted as if the writers kept switching subjects in the texts they were reading. I wanted to show them that each part of a story or nonfiction piece somehow builds on the preceding parts and that their job as readers was to try to create the text as a whole in their minds. I knew I needed to demonstrate this a number of times with a variety of genres. So I gathered up the pieces we had already looked at and planned a series of lessons. I wanted to demonstrate for them how in the midst of my reading, I often pause and ask myself how the section I'm reading connects to what came before.

On the first day of the series, I put up an excerpt from "What Pizza Delivers" again (see page 62). I started with an article because so often kids seemed to read articles as discreet sets of facts they just needed to collect. I wanted them to see that the information was designed to help them get to know more about a larger topic or to understand a bigger idea and therefore they should read it as if it all went together. I told the kids that I was going to show them how when I read, I not only try to say the text in words that make it understandable but also try to think about how each part connects to the previous parts and helps me build the whole text in my mind.

Actual Text	Think-Aloud: Putting It All Together
If you don't want to cook or eat out, a pizza is often the default. One out of every six restaurants in the U.S. is a pizzeria. Annual sales reach some $30 billion, rivaling only burger joints. And, in 1999, McDonald's purchased a pizza chain called Donato's. What does *that* tell you?	Pizza is what we eat when we want to eat at home but don't want to cook. There are tons of pizza parlors in the United States that make tons of money. Even McDonald's bought a pizza chain.
No one would dispute pizza's popularity, but when it comes to health, you often hear different stories. For many people, pizza is a lousy food, period. On the other hand, some dieticians claim that pizza is nutritious because it has components of each of the four basic food groups.	So lots of people eat pizza and this makes everyone agree that it is popular, but now there's disagreement as to whether it's healthy. Some people say it's not. Others say it is because it covers a lot of the four basic food groups.

When I finished demonstrating, I asked the kids to turn to the person next to them to try it a little bit themselves. I had them finish the section that I had started, reading it from the overhead in their heads, saying it aloud to their partner, and then asking, "How do these parts connect?" And once again, I listened in to get a sense of what they could do on a first try before sending them off to read. I reminded them that among all the strategies they reached for as they read that day, they should be sure to connect the parts of their texts and if they had trouble with the connections, they should try this strategy.

Over the next couple of days, I demonstrated the same strategy using short fiction and some essays. For the essays, I focused most of my attention on trying to help the kids see the connections between anecdotes and idea development. Often when kids read essays, they get lost in the examples and don't see how the examples illuminate the idea being explored. This strategy of looking at the big picture was very helpful for some kids.

Step Back and Reflect

Reading well means caring about the ideas in the books we read, but it also means acknowledging the role of the text and the cues it provides to help direct our meaning making. To develop a stronger relationship between my readers and the texts they were reading, I decided to make attending more closely to the texts the focus of a unit of study. Throughout this unit I demonstrated for kids what goes on in my mind as I try to build the world of the text. I paid particular attention to the things I noticed as points of difficulty for them both in my early assessment and in the work I did in response to these lessons.

As time passed, however, it became increasingly clear that in much the same way that picking and choosing across a text as opposed to building the text as a whole is problematic, it is also problematic to attend too much to the text itself. Reading is a transaction; a relationship develops between the reader and the text that defines meaning. To make sense of a text, readers bring to it more than their knowledge of the literal words on the page. They bring all of their understandings and associations to the text to provide a larger context for developing meaning than the words themselves provide. Of course this understanding isn't new. As a teacher of reading, I know that readers have to bring significant thinking to the text to make sense of it. But the reminder that came as I watched kids work was incredibly powerful. It was with this fresh reminder that I moved into the next unit of study.

Think About Your Classroom

◆ Help kids begin to attend to more of the texts they are reading by returning to a familiar text and demonstrating for the kids what it sounds like in your mind when you understand it. Using a familiar text allows the kids to focus more on your demonstration than on trying to read the story itself.

◆ Show kids how you use the same strategies for reading and thinking across genres. Do this by demonstrating not only with short stories but also with poetry, articles, and essays.

◆ Pay attention to what kids are finding difficult and turn those issues into follow-up lessons.

◆ To notice patterns of struggle in your own class, during your conferences as you explore a particular reading issue with a kid, try to think about what expert readers do and after trying a strategy with this particular student, consider whether this one moment is typical of lots of students. If so, use the story of this conference as an example for the whole class in an upcoming minilesson.

◆ If you find that kids are passing through parts of the texts that seem confusing or boring, you might teach them to interrupt their reading to retell.

◆ If you find that kids are not holding onto details of the texts that allow them to distinguish between characters or to understand how time and place move across the story, you might teach them to try to pack those details into their heads as they read.

◆ If you notice that the kids are able to talk about the parts of a text in the general order in which they occur, but don't seem to be developing a sense of how those parts fit together to make a whole, you might teach them how to regularly ask what each part has to do with the preceding parts.

···

CHAPTER 6

Figuring It Out
Making Inferences

I n the last chapter, I explored strategies for helping kids pay attention to what's literally on the page. And I ended that chapter with the reminder that reading for meaning always requires that we think about more than what is literally on the page. To consider that idea more fully, let's return for a moment to our example of "Priscilla and the Wimps" from the previous chapter.

Each time I replace the literal words on the page with words that make the text make more sense to me (see page 66), I am, in fact bringing understandings to the text that aren't literally there. When I call Monk "some kid in school," I'm thinking about the fact that the passes aren't sold by a teacher and that because typically schools are made up of teachers and kids, Monk must be a kid. When I say, "Monk didn't collect the money," I am paying attention to the fact that Monk never touched the money and realizing that not touching it in this context means that he wasn't the money collector. This act of bringing familiar contexts to this text allows me to figure out what it means.

In my classroom, I wanted to avoid teaching inference as a skill to be done outside of reading. I knew that proficient readers infer in the midst of their reading. As we make our way through a text, we figure out what's really going on and we make more of it—we develop small thoughts and opinions about the text and build on those thoughts as we read on. I wanted my students to have this skill.

Actual Text (read silently)	Saying the Text So That It Makes Sense
Listen, there was a time when you couldn't even go to the rest room around this school without a pass. And I'm not talking about those little pink tickets made out by some teacher. I'm talking about a pass that could cost anywhere up to a buck, sold by Monk Klutter.	It used to be that you couldn't even go to the bathroom without a pass sold to you by Monk Klutter, *some kid in school.*
Not that Mighty Monk ever touched money, not in public. The gang he ran, which ran the school for him, was his collection agency. They were Klutter's Kobras, a name spelled out in nailheads on six well-known black plastic windbreakers.	*Monk didn't collect the money.* No, you paid one of the Klutter's Kobras, the guys in his gang who ran the school for him. You could recognize them by the black jackets they wore with the gang name on the back.

This was especially important given what I had learned during my first assessment with "Do You Want My Opinion?" So many of the struggles kids had when reading that story showed they were not inferring well. During that assessment, I discovered that the kids hadn't been paying attention to inconsistencies in their reading and that they had changed the story to fit it into preconceived notions of the world. A study of inferential thinking in reading seemed just the way to take up these issues.

Helping students infer involves helping them understand that, in fact, we always infer—we always read more into language than what is literally spoken or written. I first began to understand this in a summer course given by Randy Bomer at the Teachers College Reading Institute a few years back. Bomer began the class with an exploration of oral language and the role of inference in our ability to communicate with each other. Through an exercise in which he wrote a series of statements on the board and had us think through our responses to those statements, Bomer helped us remember that language always carries meaning beyond the definition of the words being used and that we are able to determine this meaning by considering things outside the words, like who is saying them and the context in which they are being said. Bomer made the point that inference and interpretation are integral to our ability to negotiate our lives and we, in fact, make more of language all the time. He asked us to imagine what our relationships would be like if we had to fully explain everything we wanted others to know and understand. Communities develop shared language with which they communicate with each other and figure out what is wanted in any situation. Readers need to learn to bring the same habits of mind to literature to figure out what writers really mean in their stories.

Opening Up the Idea of Inferential Thinking for Students

I decided I, too, could help my students understand that inference was something they did every day in order to negotiate their relationships, to make their way in the world. I could then show them that in order to read inferentially, they needed to bring the same habit of mind, the same act of filling in, to their reading. Randy's strategy for helping teachers understand this idea was so compelling and clear to me that I decided to try the same activity in my room.

Reading workshop in my classroom begins very predictably each day. The students come in the room, take from their backpacks all they will need for class, put the bags in the closet or under a chair, and then gather in the meeting area for a minilesson. Same thing each day. I usually wait until about two-thirds to three-quarters of the kids are in the meeting area to begin the lesson. This lets the dawdlers know to hurry up and doesn't punish the kids who are prompt by making them wait. It also helps keep my minilessons mini, thus leaving as much time as possible for kids' actual reading.

On this particular morning I began even more quickly. I stood by the overhead projector—my usual minilesson spot—put my hands on my hips, and wrote on the overhead, "I'M WAITING!" Very quickly those who were in the meeting area threw open their literacy notebooks to the next blank spot, put the date on the top of the page, and started looking around. Those who weren't yet in the meeting area scurried to get there. Someone whispered, "What's the title of the notes?" (I require kids to take notes on minilessons and to clearly label their notes for future use.)

I let my hands drop and then asked, "What are you doing?" They looked at me with puzzled expressions. *What were they doing?* They looked around at each other. Had I finally gone crazy? One brave soul looked up at me and said, "We're getting ready for the minilesson."

"What made you do that?"

"Because we always do that."

"And what made you do it the way you did?"

"Because you said you were waiting."

"So? What does that have to do with it? Why did that make you move so fast? All I wrote was 'I'm waiting.'"

"Yeah, but that means 'Hurry up. Get into the meeting area and get ready to take notes.'"

"It does? You mean to tell me that the words *I'm waiting* mean all that? I'm not just letting you know that I'm waiting?"

The kids responded with a resounding "Yes!"

"Huh. So when your mom is standing at your apartment door with her hands on her hips and she says, 'I'm waiting,' you run to get your literacy notebook, put the date on the top of a page, and wait for the notes?"

A few giggles. Some frustration. "No! That's means 'Hurry up. We're late.'"

"It does? Really? You mean to say that sometimes the literal words *I'm waiting* mean 'Get out your lit notebook' and sometimes they mean 'We're late'? How do you know the difference?"

"Well, it has to do with who said it."

"Yeah, and where we are."

"And what else is happening."

"Ohhhhh," I said. "So you mean to tell me that literal words don't always mean what they say and that sometimes you have to think about who's saying them and where you are and what else is going on to *figure out* what they mean?"

"*Yes.*"

"And that's called *inference*. Now that your notebook is opened to the next blank page, let's take some notes to start our unit of study on inferential thinking in reading." I wrote the following on the overhead for the kids to copy:

Inference—when we bring more thinking to language in order to figure out what it really means.

I then continued by explaining that over the next few days and weeks, we were going to explore what we think about to figure out what words really mean and then we were going to try to apply that same thinking to reading in order to more fully understand our books. Before sending them off to read, I gave them the same homework assignment Bomer had given us in our summer class. I asked the kids to go home and find three examples of oral language that required them to infer. They could choose words someone said to them or to someone else or even on TV. I asked them to record their examples in the following chart:

Literal Words	What They Really Mean	How You Know
1.		
2.		
3.		

The next day in class, we shared our examples in small groups. I pulled alongside Darrin as he and his partner were discussing how in his house each night when his dad came home, his mom announced, "Darrin, Dad's home," and Darrin grabbed up his notebooks and headed to the kitchen. Apparently, in his house, "Dad's home" meant "Bring your homework to the kitchen to be checked." How did he know? Because his mom was saying it in her "mom voice" and it went like that every night.

Then I turned to Robbie. He was explaining that most nights he called Jason on the telephone and as soon as he said "Hi," Jason started rattling off the homework for the night. Jason and Robbie were not good friends.

Jason knew that when Robbie called, it was only because he didn't know the homework and knew that Jason would.

While it was fun and interesting to share our examples, it was more important to get at the thinking behind our meaning making, so when I gathered the kids back together for a large-group share, I focused our attention on the third column of our homework chart. We came up with the following incomplete list of questions that help people think about what literal language really means:

Have I ever heard of this before?

Who's speaking? Why might she or he be saying this now?

What might this sound like?

What was said before?

Where does this take place?

What's really going on here?

Has this ever happened before?

How does this situation go?

When is this happening?

Who's the reference? What might this be referring to?

Have I experienced this before?

What might this want me to do?

What's the context of this comment?

Is this supposed to be funny, threatening, sarcastic (and so on)?

Is there more in the text that I might use?

With this work in mind, over the next few days, I turned the class' attention to reading. I wanted the kids to understand that when we read, we apply the same kind of thinking to figure out what the texts really mean, what's really going on in them. I also wanted to do a little teacher research myself. I knew that there were going to be some pitfalls—places where the kids would struggle or misapply the thinking. So I set up some structures in the class that would allow me to see inside what the kids were doing.

Using Think-Alouds to Demonstrate Inferential Thinking

Because I wanted the kids to see as explicitly as possible what proficient reading looks like, I began this unit like I do many others—by demonstrating the work as a whole. This allows the kids to get a sense of the big picture. Remember, I want kids to understand that reading is not really made up of a list of skills that you do; rather, it involves a way of thinking that allows you to make rich meaning of the words on the page. I want kids to see that this work happens as you're reading, not after you've read the words on the page.

For my demonstrations, I chose a short stack of texts, both fiction and nonfiction, that offered a variety of issues readers needed to deal with to make sense of them fully. I then copied excerpts from the texts onto transparencies and each day for a number of days, I put the texts up on the overhead. On the first day, my minilesson went like this:

> So, over the past few days, we have been exploring what it means to infer. We have looked at language that we use and hear in our everyday lives and realized that often the literal words we say mean something totally different than their definitions. We have realized that people need to bring more thinking than just definitions to language to understand what is really being said. We have called this thinking *inference*. Today, I want to begin demonstrating for you how I bring the same kind of thinking to my reading. I have a short excerpt from "Moonbeam Dawson and the Killer Bear," by Jean Davies Okimoto (1989). I am going to read it to myself and demonstrate for you the inferential thinking I do as I read. Your job is to watch me in a way that will allow you to describe what I'm doing so that you can begin to do it more thoughtfully in your own reading.

I put the text up on the overhead and thought aloud (my thinking appears in italics).

Excerpt from "Moonbeam Dawson and the Killer Bear"

Moonbeam Dawson got sick of explaining about his name. [*"Oh, people didn't understand something about his name."*] The problem [*"with his name"*] was at its worst during the height of the salmon season when the lodge was loaded with guests. [*"What does salmon season at the lodge have to do with his name?"*] Once, he'd thought of making a tape. [*"He'd make a tape recording of some sort."*] He'd have a miniature electronic gadget, like James Bond might have [*"The spy in the movies, 007—he always had these cool gadgets for spying and communicating."*], and he'd casually flick a tiny switch hidden on his pants, in the pocket or something. Maybe on his belt. [*"He'd respond in a cool way like James Bond."*] So when some guest said, "Moonbeam? You're kidding! Moonbeam! How'd a guy get a name like Moonbeam?!" he'd flick the switch, the tape would come on, and he'd go about his business, busing tables, or pouring water. He wouldn't even have to look up. [*"So if a guest of the hotel—someone staying there—started asking him how he got his name, he'd turn the tape on and it would explain while he continued working—oh, he works at the lodge. That's what his name has to do with the lodge. The height of the salmon season means more guests and then more people ask him about his name. He'd rather turn the tape on over and over than explain it guest after guest."*]

When I was done with the excerpt, I asked the kids to turn to the person next to them and talk about what I had done. They offered the following explanations:

"You say what's going on in the text."

"You figure out who it's about—like who the *he*s and *she*s are."

"You kind of explain what the stuff in the story means?"

"You kind of think about the same things we said when we did our homework last week—like who's here and where they are and where you've heard this stuff before."

I ended my minilesson by telling them that over the next few days I would be demonstrating this work with a variety of texts, and during work time as I conferred, I was going to ask them to think aloud so I could see what they did as they tried to read inferentially. This setup allowed me to research how kids applied and misapplied these ideas and to figure out what to teach in future minilessons.

Early Discoveries

The kids' work on inference during both collaborative reading and independent reading revealed some of the same patterns of reading and misreading I had discovered in my earlier assessments. As I moved from student to student and group to group, however, new patterns emerged as well. These new ways of reading showed quite a lot about what they did well—what they understood about reading fully and thoughtfully—but also showed what was leading them to limited or incorrect understandings.

Turning on Their Minds

First and foremost, there was a fundamental difference between kids who read with their minds on and kids who didn't. Many kids talked about getting immersed in the story—about their ability to see and hear the characters in their minds. Others, however, struggled to talk about their books when asked to do so in a conference. My first instinct was to check whether their books were simply too difficult. And while this was the case for a number of kids, for others, the problem was that they were just not attending to the text as they read. It was as if their minds were shut off as their eyes went down the page.

Sometimes I could see this kind of reading just by watching some kids from afar. During a conference, I might look across the room and see a student with a book held fairly far from her face, looking anywhere but at the book. Other kids were not so obvious in the way they glazed over their books. Glen was one such kid. Often, when I pulled alongside Glen for a conference and asked him to tell me about the part of the book he was reading in a way that would make it clear to me, he did one of two things. Either he gave me a book-jacket-type summary or he gave a vague explanation that skirted around the chapter he was in. When I asked him to talk about the part he was working on now, he just looked at me blankly. Fundamental to this inference work, therefore, was continued work on developing reading for understanding, not just word calling or avoiding.

Paying Attention to Changes in the Text

I also noticed a difference between kids who paid attention to changes in the texts and those who didn't. Lots of kids recognized when new characters were being introduced and paid attention to their relationships with characters they already knew. But other kids acted as if they were reading a different book when someone new was introduced.

Similarly, some kids were very skilled at understanding how and why writers moved their stories through time in the ways they did. They recognized skips in time and flashbacks and were able to explain what would make the characters think back on earlier times in their lives when they did. Other kids did not pay attention to these moves. They seemed to read as if every moment were in the present and characters jumped from place to place. They did not accumulate the text in a way that would build the story as a whole and allow them to glean any thinking from it. These same kids also read each word as if it carried the same weight, not understanding that, often, individual word choice creates subtle shifts in meaning.

Revising Prior Knowledge

Finally, I noticed that often kids *over*applied prior knowledge. This was tricky to resolve. In a way it was exactly what I wanted from them—I wanted them to use what they knew from outside of a text to figure out what was really going on in the story. Unfortunately, lots of kids did not do this in a way that opened up the story and created possibilities; they did it in a way that limited or twisted the stories they were reading, often because of stereotypes they had about the world. For example, if in a contemporary young adult novel, the characters' actions were different from their own, they said it was not a "city story." "Oh, that's what it's like in the country," they'd say.

Categories of Inference

Throughout this research time, I took copious notes, trying to figure out how to shape the next part of the curriculum. I needed a way to name what I was seeing and talk to the kids about it so I could teach explicitly and thoughtfully into what I saw them doing. So I spent a couple of hours after school one day rereading my notes and trying to create categories around which I could organize my teaching.

I quickly realized that I could organize my lessons into two big categories—in general, two different kinds of inference. The first I began to call Figure It Out inferences and the second I called Making More inferences.

Figure It Out inferences are those inferences the reader needs in order to make sense of what is really happening in the story. Without them the text is really incomprehensible. These inferences include, but are not limited to

- figuring out who's in the story, where they are, and what's really going on
- figuring out what the characters are really doing, saying, and thinking
- figuring out grammatical references
- figuring out how and why time and place are moving the way they are

Making More inferences are those that enrich a reading of the story. I describe the work we did with this category in the next chapter, but for now it's important to know that these inferences include, but are not limited to

- making more of what the characters do, say, and think (thinking about their personalities, motivations, internal conflicts, etc.)
- making more of the time and place in which the story occurs
- considering the symbolism of names, titles, objects, colors, numbers, shapes, and other details

- developing theories about the writer's values and beliefs at moments in the text
- thinking about fairness at moments in the text
- making personal connections

It's important to remember that these categories are of course arbitrary and there's plenty of crossover, but it was a helpful way to divide up the teaching—to figure out a plan for instruction and minilessons.

Figure It Out Minilessons

I began the next set of minilessons with a series of Figure It Out lessons. It made sense to start here because it felt like an extension of all the work we had done in the last unit of study on attending to more of the text. I organized these minilessons in the same way I designed the lessons for the previous unit of study. The kids gathered in the meeting area, typically around an overhead projector. I explained and then demonstrated or showed examples of what I wanted them to understand. They talked about it with each other or tried it out a little for themselves, then took some notes to maintain a record for themselves. Then they went off around the room to continue their ongoing reading work, incorporating the day's teaching into what they were doing. And I, of course, spent their work time making my way around the room, conducting reading conferences.

Recognizing Shifts in Time and Place

One lesson I taught involved helping the kids think about how time and place move across a story. I began this minilesson by explaining to the kids "When I read and I'm trying to build the world of a story in my head, it's important to have a sense of time and place. And I don't just mean that I can name when and where the story takes place, but more that I understand how time and place are moving across the story and how that movement contributes to the meaning of the story. Many of the books you are reading do not move chronologically through time. The writers use a variety of techniques to play with time as a way to make the characters and the situations they are in more complex. Today I'd like to show you an example of what I mean and talk you through some thinking that demonstrates how I make sense of this. Your job is to watch in a way that will make you able to apply similar thinking to your own reading."

I then put up on the overhead an excerpt (see page 78) from Maria Testa's short story "Family Day" (1995). I had read it aloud earlier in the year, and I reminded the kids that it's the story of a family that spends its Sundays visiting the father in prison. I then asked them to look at the section I had on the overhead, in which Anthony, who is telling the story, describes the waiting area of the jail. I told the kids that I wanted them to listen to the way I focused on time and place as I read to myself and thought aloud for them.

After I had the kids share with their neighbors what they noticed about what I'd just done, we spent a few minutes deciding what to write in our notes so that we would remember this lesson and could refer to it when we needed it later. We talked about noticing the way the writer used a different font to indicate the change and how italics typically indicate internal thinking. We also talked about the parallel time cues—the fact that the present scene and the flashback were both Sundays. This could help us figure out what was going on. I ended the lesson by telling the kids that they needed to read their own books in a way that would allow them to make greater sense of the movement through time and place across their books.

Rethinking Misunderstandings

Along with helping the kids see examples of inferential thinking in action, I wanted to explicitly teach lessons that addressed some of the problems they were having. One such struggle was that they often held onto previous knowledge or understandings even when parts of a story should have made them reconsider their thinking. I wanted the kids to understand that often when we read, we need to consider our knowledge as a possibility and be willing to revise it when the text challenges what we think we understand.

To teach this, I gathered the kids together and put a copy of Shirley Jackson's "The Lottery" (1982) on the overhead. I had read the story to the

Actual Text	My Think-Aloud
The waiting room is hell. I suppose this is true of the waiting room in any prison, but I only know about our prison. They should probably call it the Eternal Waiting Room From Hell, because on Sunday, you have to wait for an eternity. I guess every mother in the world shares Mamma's view of Sundays; the waiting room is always filled with families. . . . *"Let's talk," Daddy says, as we flop on the grass in the backyard. "It's good for a father and son to talk." I smile and close my eyes as the sun warms my face. It's Sunday afternoon, and I'm wearing new jeans and a red baseball cap.*	So it's Sunday. They've gone to the prison to visit their dad. Now they're sitting in the waiting room, which is crowded with lots of other families. Now the text changes. Anthony and his dad are lying in the grass in their yard on Sunday afternoon. Dad wants to talk to him. It feels like the text has just switched topics, but I know as a reader that the parts have to connect. So I'm thinking about what clues are here to help me make the connection. The text is in italics, which I know often means that the character is thinking, and I also know they are no longer in the prison waiting room. Oh, this must be a flashback. Anthony is sitting in the waiting room on a Sunday and he flashes back in his mind to other Sundays before his dad was in prison. I guess the reason he does so is because he doesn't like to spend his Sundays at the prison and he's remembering better times when he spent his Sundays talking with his dad at home.

kids earlier in the year. "The Lottery" is about a community whose answer to ensuring that there is enough food and resources for everyone is to hold a lottery each year in which the "winner" gets stoned by the citizens. The story takes place on lottery day when all the villagers gather together to find out who will "win." Mr. Summers calls out family names one by one, and heads of families come up to take a slip of paper. The one with a mark is the winner. Then each family member picks a slip and the winner of this round is stoned. I began the lesson by explaining to the kids that I had noticed that while they were reading, some of the confusions they were having were coming from rigid thinking. They were holding onto understandings without revising when a story asked them to. Then I told them I wanted to show them what I meant by looking at "The Lottery."

"I want you to watch the way I revisit the story and notice how I let the details of the text make me rethink my initial understanding."

Rethinking Misunderstandings

OK, so I begin by looking at the title: "The Lottery." I know what a lottery is. People buy tickets to win money. Typically, you can get them at the drugstore or stationery store and then you watch TV to see if the number on your ticket is the one that comes up. That means you're the winner—you get the money. So, the story is going to be something about that.

I begin reading, and immediately, by the second sentence, I need to rethink. Let's look at that sentence. "The people of the village began to gather in the square, between the post office and the bank, around 10 o'clock; in some towns there were so many people that the lottery took two days and had to be started on June 26th, but in this village, where there were only about three hundred people, the whole lottery took less than two hours, so it could begin at ten o'clock in the morning and still be through in time to allow the villagers to get home for noon dinner." So this seems different. I wonder why the town gathers together for the lottery. This is somehow not like the lottery that I know. I don't quite understand yet what this lottery is, but I do know it's different; I have to let go a little of what I think I know and keep reading.

And so I get to the part where Mr. Summers, who is conducting the lottery, sets up the black box and stool and begins stirring the papers inside. I think to myself, "OK, maybe this is similar, but maybe the story takes place in a time and place when the technology for conducting lotteries the way we do didn't exist." I keep reading and get to the part where Mr. Summers explains that he will read the names of all the heads of families and then "the men [will] come up and take a paper out of the box." He tells them "Keep the paper folded in your hand without looking at it until everyone [has] a turn." OK, it's different again. In this lottery, everyone in the village participates. Around here, you participate only if you want to buy a ticket.

I then turned off the overhead projector and asked the kids to turn to their neighbors and talk about what they noticed about what I'd just demonstrated. After a minute or two, I asked a couple of kids to share their ideas with the group. In the end, we decided to record in our notebooks that when we read, we cannot hold onto our previous knowledge so tightly that it makes us confused about what's going on in a story. We have to be willing to let the details of a story help us rethink and therefore figure out what's really going on. I then asked the kids to pay particular attention to this idea as they were reading independently and told them I'd talk more about this in my conferences over the next few days and weeks.

Step Back and Reflect

As I have worked to help kids make sense of the texts they were reading and to care about getting them, one question has been burning in my head: Does it really matter? That is, does it really matter whether kids get it right, whether they absolutely understand what the text literally says and what's really happening with great accuracy moment to moment and point to point through the pages? After all, we all miscue sometimes.

Reading is a transaction between the reader and the text, and we are always reading the text we create rather than the actual text on the page (Rosenblatt 1978). In both large and small ways, we make the text we are reading into something other than what's there. Sometimes we need to revise our thinking because we realize the text has become incomprehensible. We realize that we don't understand something that's happening. We go back and reread and realize we missed something or misread something and we fix up our reading. But probably equally as often, we misread and we don't fix up. We turn the text into something that's not quite there. Does it really matter? After all, there are no reading police coming to arrest us for misreading. No one is testing us to see whether we got all the details right. Who cares? It's our own independent reading, right?

In fact, it does matter. It matters because it is the details that stir the imagination. While I am not arguing against miscues and the fact that they often do not represent reading misunderstandings, I do want to argue that one of the major reasons—I hope *the* major reason—we read is to let books lead us to think about our lives and the world in which we live. This is not a small thing. We read to invent lives for ourselves, to reimagine the world around us. Wolfgang Iser (1974) says that the novel was invented to allow us to explore social norms. Often novels are written in opposition to social conventions of the day in order to provide us with a context to explore the world in which we live and to rethink the way that world works. If this is the case, I want to read and I want my kids to read in a way that will allow us to do this well. And I believe we can do this by paying attention to the details.

To read well in a small way is to say, "Oh, this is one of those books about teen love," or "This is about how racism is bad." To read well in a big way, however, is to move beyond these first, quick ideas and to figure out how the text positions us to think about these issues. Readers who are trying to read in this way might ask themselves, "What does this text say to me about teen love or racism?" Answering this question requires that we lean in and read closely, that we pay attention to what's really going on in the stories we are reading and think about the symbolism of the details (see Chapter 7 for more about symbolism). In this way, *trying* to get it right, *trying* to read in a way that will build a rich story world full of meaning, matters most of all.

Think About Your Classroom

◆ Figuring out a text means recognizing that there's more to the text than what is literally on the page. Begin by helping kids understand that they infer all the time. You might do this by studying oral language. The kids might collect examples of language that requires them to infer from TV, in school, and at home. They might also begin with examples of texts that are very familiar to them to realize how much inferring they do as they read.

◆ Another way to help kids think about inference is to look at their writing. A writing strategy like "show, don't tell," in which kids work on trying to show how the people in their pieces are feeling or acting, helps kids develop a feel for inference as readers.

◆ Help kids transfer what they learn in the early part of this study by naming the kinds of thinking they use to figure out what the literal words they hear or write really mean and then demonstrate how to use that same thinking as they read.

◆ Organize inferences into categories to avoid letting your lessons jump around. You might help your kids think about those inferences they need to really *figure out* what is actually going on in the text they are reading and those that help them *make more* of the text. Remember that these do not represent a hierarchy of inference, but rather a way to organize teaching.

◆ As you confer, notice the ways in which kids struggle to infer and plan follow-up demonstration lessons that will focus on those particular difficulties. Not every struggle needs to become a minilesson. Often a student has trouble with a particular text in ways that don't really need to be shared or explored with the whole class. In minilessons, focus on those issues that repeatedly show up in many students' inferences.

◆ If you find that students are struggling to recognize shifts in time and place, try to find a text that can provide an explicit example of how to think through these shifts and demonstrate that thinking for the students.

◆ If you find that students are developing misunderstandings as they build the world of a text and are holding onto those misunderstandings as they continue to read, even in the face of contradictory evidence, teach them how to revise their thinking as they read.

CHAPTER 7

Making More of the Text

Creating Interpretations

Learning to Take a Story Out into the World: A Rationale

Every year, there comes a point in my teaching when the kids outwardly resist the curriculum. They simply reject the work we're doing. They tell me, "I don't want to write thoughts on sticky notes. They get in the way. They slow me down. I want to just read." For some, this resistance comes early in the year, and I deal with it in the conferences. But every year, without fail, there is always a moment when it feels as if the entire class is rejecting the work we're doing. Everyone wants to keep reading without interruption, without pushing his or her thinking.

I find myself questioning the work also. Isn't simply loving to read or even just wanting to turn the pages good enough? After all, the desire to keep turning the pages, to get to the end and find out what happens, is often the primary force in reading (Mackey 1997). And probably, often enough, that quick reading does affect the way we think and live. There are probably times when we read quickly and something strikes our subconscious and we find ourselves thinking about it later—maybe we even let it affect decisions we make.

But just when I am about to convince myself that maybe just giving the kids more time to fall in love with their books is good enough, I am reminded why reading *thoughtfully* matters. Last summer when I was reading the fifth

Harry Potter book, *Harry Potter and the Order of the Phoenix* (Rowling 2003), I was reminded once again.

The Order of the Phoenix arrived on the shelves at the perfect time for me. The school year had just ended and while I was busy preparing to teach at an institute on the teaching of reading at Teachers College, I was looking for an escape. I am a notorious procrastinator, and computer solitaire was losing its effect. Harry Potter seemed the perfect alternative. My first thought, as I began reading, was that it would be great escapist reading. I figured I'd curl up with the book and just let the story carry me into another world. I couldn't wait to be taken back to quidditch games and Hagrid's animals and to find out how Voldemort would return. I couldn't wait to get lost in the adventure, the excitement of it all. And it did begin just the way I expected. Right from the start, dementors attack Harry and Dudley, and Harry is threatened with expulsion from Hogwarts for using magic around muggles. And I was gone.

Then I read Chapter 11, about two hundred pages into the book. In Chapter 11, I was officially introduced to Professor Umbridge, the new Defense of the Dark Arts teacher. Those of you who are fans might remember that Defense of the Dark Arts has been a struggling class at Hogwarts. A new teacher has been needed each year. And this year, it's Professor Umbridge. When I got to this part, I realized this was not actually the first I had heard of Professor Umbridge. I had met her about a hundred pages earlier at Harry's expulsion hearing in front of the Ministry of Magic. Professor Umbridge is Delores Umbridge, senior undersecretary to the Minister of Magic—a government employee. And now here on page 213 I met her again, this time as Professor Umbridge. It turned out that she had been appointed by the Ministry of Magic to teach at Hogwarts—a noneducator appointed by the government to teach. Hmmm. A red flag went up in my mind.

In Chapter 11, Professor Umbridge gives a little speech to the students. While most are deaf to Umbridge's words, Hermione pays close attention, and I found that I paid close attention as well. Professor Umbridge talks about how the Ministry of Magic has always considered education of utmost importance. She talks about how each of the headmasters at Hogwarts has brought something new to the school but says that while some of this progress has been worthy, some of it has been progress for progress' sake. It's time the school reevaluated all this progress, she declares. It's time to find *balance*—balance between tradition and innovation.

By this point I was sitting up in bed and my mind was spinning. This was beginning to sound very familiar. I tried to ignore this and read on—this was supposed to be escapist reading. I was supposed to be procrastinating. But two pages later I realized I was really no longer reading. I had no idea what had just happened on those two pages. I was no longer thinking about Harry Potter. I was thinking about all of us and the world in which we find ourselves. I was thinking about the calls for balance in our school systems. I was thinking about the so-called reading wars created by politicians and corporations to push an educational agenda that would sell more textbooks and more standardized tests.

I continued to read, this time holding onto these connections. I didn't want to let them go. Well, things went from bad to worse at Hogwarts. First Umbridge transformed the Defense of the Dark Arts class into a theory class. The kids would no longer be doing magic, no longer be practicing defense of the Dark Arts; they would just be reading silently out of the textbook. Apparently Umbridge believed that if the kids knew the theory, they would be prepared should they ever need the skills—hmmm. And then Umbridge was appointed High Inquisitor of Hogwarts, a job that gave her quite a bit more power. Not only was she now in the role of formally observing and evaluating her colleagues, thus deciding who was fit to teach and who was not, but she was also governing life at Hogwarts. She banned all student groups at school—teams, clubs, and so on—that didn't get explicit permission from her to keep operating. She declared that teachers could not discuss anything with students except content connected to the subject that they taught. And after a newspaper reporter interviewed Harry, she declared that students were no longer allowed to read that newspaper.

I thought to myself, "How will the community respond?" I just knew Harry and his friends would offer up an answer, a way to think about our own situation. You see we, too, are living in a time when decisions that affect our lives are being made without our input, without thoughtful dialogue and debate. Decisions about how we should teach and what constitutes sound educational research are being made based on what appear to be quick fixes rather than an acknowledgment of the complexity of the challenges we face. I read on with this big question in mind—what can communities do when faced with powerful bureaucracies that disregard and dismiss them?

In response to Umbridge's teaching, the kids worked outside the system and formed their own secret Defense of the Dark Arts class. Led by Harry, they practiced magic that would hone their skills and prepare them for times when they would need to defend themselves. And the grown-ups reconstituted an old organization called the Order of the Phoenix (OOP), a secret organization charged with fighting Voldemort, the Dark Lord. The characters in the story also worked inside the system. Many of the grown-ups inside the OOP continued to teach at Hogwarts or work at the Ministry of Magic. They didn't quit those positions and distance themselves from the government structures. They stayed connected; they worked on the inside, perhaps with the hopes of effecting change in those structures.

Reading this Harry Potter book, I couldn't help but let my mind slip out of the story and into my own world—not just my personal world but the political world in which I live. Even when I set myself up to read just to get lost in the story, my mind pushed itself into making larger connections. And I couldn't just stop at those connections. I couldn't just name them and move on. I had to make more of them. I had to articulate them clearly in my mind. I had to raise questions about how the text might position me to think about these connections. I had to find words to answer those questions, not just in the book but also in my world. This matters for me as a reader.

When we read, we make meaning of the print on the page. The meaning we make is informed by our experiences and identity and other texts we have read (Rosenblatt 1978). When we read, each new text supports our understanding of the next text (Fielding and Pearson 1994). When we talk, each conversation enriches the way we think about the next poem or novel or biography. Very often, when I pull alongside the kids in my class and ask them to talk about what's going on in their minds while they read, they tell me that they are seeing the story in their minds. They are imagining the characters and the scenes in which the story is taking place. The most engaged readers describe this imagining with energy and passion—the joy of reading is getting lost in the world of the story.

But too often, the imagining that kids do is left on the pages of the text. The experience ends with the last word on the last page. The kids rarely think to take the characters and their stories out of the text and into their own world. They rarely use reading to imagine possibilities for themselves, to envision not just the world of the story but also a new and better world for themselves.

To help kids learn to read in this way means to teach them the habits of mind not just of proficient readers but of critical readers. My goal is not just to make the kids want to read and able to read but to help them see reading as a context to examine social issues. It means teaching them to carry in their minds a set of critical questions that readers use when trying to think about social issues. Critical readers examine the language and ideas inside the books they read. Critical readers become personally connected to the books they are reading, but they also let their reading help them examine larger connections between their personal experiences and the social and political systems in which we all participate (Edelsky 1999).

I knew, however, that this work would be difficult. At the same time that middle schoolers are powerfully interested in issues of fairness and justice, they also resist ideas that challenge their sense of order in the world. It was this conflict, along with my belief that this work is of the utmost importance, that made me forge ahead.

What Issues Are Hiding in This Text?

To help kids develop the habits of mind of critical readers, I designed a unit of study that would teach them to simply name and then explore the big issues that lived behind the words in their books. I began this unit of study by telling the kids that I wanted to share with them a "reading secret." I told them, "It is one of those big ideas about reading that is the reason that many people read. Today we're going to begin a study that helps us understand this secret. Are you ready? Here goes. There are *issues* hiding in the books we read. Not only are there stories and information that we can come to know and think about in small ways, but there are also opportunities to think about ideas that are important to us—ideas that help us imagine ways to live and what we might believe to be just and true in the world.

"Today, I want to show you how I begin to name the issues that are hiding in texts as I read. I have here a text that we've read before; it is Beth's poem. Today as I reread it, I'm going to try to ask myself what large concepts might be hiding here and I'm going to write those in the margins of the text. Watch how I do that.

"First I am going to read the poem through to get a sense of it as a whole. While I am reading, listen in a way that reminds you of previous conversations we've had about it. When I'm done reading, turn and talk to the person next to you to share your thinking."

Internet Poetry
The girl writes,
She looks up,
glancing across
her classmates' faces.
They are indifferent,
graced with worried concentration,
Her own expression that of
one near tears,
perpetually.
Enhancing it, perhaps
to see if anyone will notice.
Of course,
no one does.
Sighing softly,
she lowers her head
back to her poem.

"I write of sunbeams
falling from the sky,
and of a chickadee
learning how to fly.
I write of rosebuds
With just a hint of dew,
But no matter what I write of,
I always write of you."

After giving the kids a minute to talk to their neighbors, I continued. "Now I'm going to read it again and I am going to try to think about issues that might be hiding in the text. Remember an issue is an idea. It won't be in the text literally. It's sort of floating behind the words, and when we read the text, we find ourselves thinking about it. We might think about this as idea topics the poem helps us explore. Watch how I read the poem and try to name some possibilities. I'll jot them in the margins as I think of them."

I reread the poem in a lower voice this time to model how I read to myself and then began to name some issues. "Well, I see gender. Remember, that's maleness and femaleness. And I see growing up, ideas about adolescent development, and identity. I bet a lot of you are beginning to see some issues here too. Why don't you turn to the person next to you and share what you are thinking?" After a few minutes I asked the kids to share their ideas with the group and add them to the list I had started.

Sean called out first. "Respect."

Then Carrie. "Fitting in."

Then more kids called out their ideas.

"Peer pressure."

"Love."

"Image."

"School."

And then I continued. "Today when you go off to read, try to keep this question in your mind: What issues are hiding in the text I'm reading? Keep a sticky note in your book to jot them down. That way you can work with them as you read on and we can talk about them in conferences."

As the kids went off, I turned to the list we made and began thinking about whether or not the ideas they named were really issues at all. What even makes something an issue versus a topic? As I looked at the list I realized that they were, in fact, all ideas—they all allowed us to think abstractly and develop an interpretation. They weren't, however, all social issues. By that I mean they weren't all ideas through which we could not only examine the text but also use the text to help us examine those ideas in our world. Some, like gender, clearly were social issues. We could examine the text through the lens of our understandings of gender and use the text to examine the world. Others, like school and identity, were merely abstractions through which we could develop interpretations of the text.

For now, I did not want to raise this distinction with the class. It would only complicate things. I wanted to begin with a sense of openness. I wanted the kids to feel like they could go off and try to think about their books in more abstract ways. Over the next few days, as I demonstrated again and again with a variety of texts, I incorporated examples from the kids' independent reading in my lessons. And together we developed a big list of issues we were finding in our texts. The kids began to develop a sense of which of those were social issues and which were simply abstractions.

Among all the things I wanted the kids to understand, two stood out as most important. The first was that there was more than one issue hiding in the texts they were reading. Their job was to consider possible ideas worth exploring, not to think that there is always one main idea. I knew that later I would need to help them understand that some ideas are more interesting or compelling than others, but for now it was important simply to break down the notion that a book has a single idea and that the reader's only job is to find it and name it. Therefore, every time we tried to name issues in our texts, we always pushed ourselves to consider more than one.

Secondly, I wanted the kids to get beyond simply naming issues that were in their books. I wanted them to understand that the books we read position us to think about those issues in particular ways. It's not just that Beth's poem is about gender or adolescence or peer relationships but that she positions us to think about each of these in particular ways. Hiding beneath her words are ways of thinking about the issues her poem addresses. Helping kids see how texts position us to think would begin to help them see that these issues are not simple, black-and-white ideas and would set the stage for later work in developing complexity of thought. I knew, therefore, that I had to begin with a set of minilessons that would address this.

What Might *This* Text Want Me to Think About *This* Issue?

I began teaching kids how to consider how a text positions us on an idea by returning to Beth's poem.

"Over the past few days we have been trying to read in a way that will allow us to think about and name the issues that are hiding in the texts we read. Today I want to push that work one step further by helping you understand that it is not enough to name the issues. We must also consider the many different ways in which the texts want us to think about these ideas. Today I want to show you how I ask and then try to answer the following question of Beth's poem: What might this poem say to me about identity? I chose that issue because I think it is one of the more interesting ones on the list, not because it is any more 'correct' than any of the others. I am going to reread the poem, and as I do, I'm going to try to think about this question. As I do so, I want you to watch in a way that will make you able to try it yourself in your own reading. I'm going to ask you to try a bit with the person sitting next to you before we go off for independent reading today."

I then turned to the poem and read it quietly to myself. When I was done, I paused for a moment to consider my answer, and then I said, "Well, perhaps the poem says to me that young people hide their true feelings even when they don't want to. Sometimes, in quiet ways, young people try to show their feelings, but when they are ignored, they hide behind a more acceptable identity. It seems, though, that the poem suggests that this is not the isolated feeling of just one person. Maybe there are social forces at work here that define just how far this person should push to be noticed."

As I spoke, I wrote my ideas on the overhead to help the kids internalize my example. Then I turned to them and said, "Turn to the person next to you. First talk for a minute about what you noticed I did, then practice for a moment with your partner using the book you are reading."

As the kids tried to articulate how their texts might have been positioning them to think about an issue, I scooted around to try to get a sense of what they were and were not understanding. What I noticed here, along with my observations during conferences, informed the lessons I taught over the next few days.

Fitting into an Issue World

The next step was to help the students understand that while many texts explore the same issues, it doesn't mean they position us to think about them in the same way. Each issue—race, gender, class, social development, and so on—has many facets. I often tell the kids in my class that each of these issues lives in a world. The world of an issue is made up of everything that's ever been said, written, sung, thought, uttered, seen, and so on about that issue. As readers, we need to think about where the particular text we are reading fits into the "issue world." What does it say to us compared with other texts that explore the same issue?

To teach this, I decided to take two texts that explore the same issue and show the kids how the texts position us to think about the issue in different ways. I chose two early picture books, *Farmer Duck*, by Martin Waddell (1991) and *Click, Clack, Moo: Cows That Type*, by Doreen Cronin (2000). I chose them because they are very clear examples of how two texts can get you to think differently about the same issue.

These two stories are both about animals organizing themselves to respond to unjust working conditions on their farms. I began this work with two minilessons during which I read the texts aloud and, as a group, we considered what issues were hiding in the texts. Then, on the third day, I began a minilesson by putting up an overhead with excerpts from the books (see page 93):

Farmer Duck by Martin Waddell	Click, Clack Moo: Cows That Type by Doreen Cronin
The hens and the cow and the sheep got very upset. They loved the duck. So they held a meeting under the moon, and they made a plan for the morning. [The cow, the sheep, and the hens crept into the farmer's house and they] squeezed under the bed of the farmer and wriggled about. The bed started to rock and the farmer woke up, and he called "How goes the work?" and . . . "Moo!" "Baa!" "Cluck!" They lifted his bed and he started to shout and they banged and they bounced the old farmer about and about and about, right out of the bed . . . And he fled . . .	The cows held an emergency meeting. All night long, Farmer Brown waited for an answer. Duck knocked on the door early the next morning. He handed Farmer Brown a note: Dear Farmer Brown: We will exchange our type-writer for electric blankets. Leave them outside the barn door and we will send Duck over with the typewriter. Sincerely, The Cows Farmer Brown decided this was a good idea . . .

I began, "I have on the overhead an excerpt from *Farmer Duck,* by Martin Waddell. You'll remember that it is the story of a duck that lives on the farm of a lazy farmer. All day long the duck does all the work and the farmer stays in bed. The duck's animal friends feel so bad for the duck that they call a meeting. The animals decide the only way to respond to the farmer's abuse is to sneak into his house and throw him out. And that's what they do. In the end all the animals decide to do the work together.

"Next to that I have an excerpt from *Click, Clack, Moo: Cows That Type,* by Doreen Cronin. Remember that it is the story of a group of cows that write a letter to the farmer requesting electric blankets for themselves and the hens to fight off the cold in the barn. When the farmer says no, they go on strike—no milk or eggs for the farmer to sell. Instead of convincing the farmer to provide electric blankets, this makes the farmer mad. So the cows hold an emergency meeting and decide to negotiate with the farmer. If the farmer provides the blankets, they will give up the typewriter on which they have been writing him notes. The farmer decides this is a good deal and makes the trade. In the end, the ducks, who up until then had been a neutral party, type a note requesting a diving board for the pond. Of course the farmer agrees.

"OK. So watch how I try to talk about the different ways these two stories position me to think about the same issue. First, I'll try to name the idea they seem to share. They are both about how workers respond to what they see as unjust working conditions. I think I will look at them from the perspective of the workers and suggest that they both want me to think something about what to do in the face of injustice. Then, I'll try to think about how they are different. *Farmer Duck* seems to want me to think that the way to respond is to overthrow the boss and if workers get together, they can do just that. The animals all join forces to run the lazy farmer off the farm. *Click, Clack, Moo,* however, is a bit different. It wants me to think, perhaps, that rather than overthrow the boss when he doesn't comply with your wishes, you should strike. That's what the cows decided they would do. Instead of running the farmer off the farm like the animals did in the other book, they went on strike."

I then turned back to the kids. "To try this out a bit, please turn to the person next to you and talk a little about how the book you are reading makes you think about any of the big ideas you see in it. You might try to push yourself by talking also how it compares with the ways others might want you to think about the issue. I'll take this work up more in the days to come and in my conferences."

Putting the Pieces Together: Staying Afloat

Teaching often feels like running back and forth across a ship. Anytime I lean into one idea, the ship tips and the other ideas scatter. Sometimes, however, instead of running to the other side of the ship to recover the missing ideas, I need to run to the middle. I do so in an attempt to connect new strategies to the ideas with which we've been working. Moving between thinking about big issues across a book and focusing on the details that help you explore those ideas requires a balancing act.

Considering how a text positions us to think about a particular issue, therefore, involves paying attention to the details of the text. It is in the details of the text, in the character's actions, thoughts, and words and the writer's choice of words when describing or explaining a situation, that a more extensive way of thinking about big ideas can be found. In order to deepen the kids' work, I knew I needed to make this connection explicit for them. Therefore, I decided it was time to bring our attention back to inferential thinking. But this time, we'd focus on Making More inferences—those needed to *enhance our reading* of a story and therefore allow us to move out of the story and into a vision of our own worlds. The details of a text can help us find possible ways to act and think for ourselves.

Making More of the Characters in the Text

The first Making More lesson I taught focused on characters. Characters play roles in stories. Paying attention to their words and actions helps us think about their roles and therefore might give clues to how the text might want us to think. I wanted the kids to see how I try to develop some thinking about characters as I read. I began by returning to Shirley Jackson's "The Lottery." I put it up on the overhead and told the kids that I was going to think aloud in front of them again. This time, I was going to try to think about the characters, specifically about what kind of people they were—their motivations, their struggles, their personality traits—for the purpose of thinking more about the big ideas I saw hiding in the story.

I began by reminding the kids that the last time we had looked at the text, they had talked about how it seemed to be exploring issues of community. They said the story got them to think about how communities decide to make sacrifices for the larger good and that sometimes those sacrifices feel extreme. They ended the conversation by wondering whether the sacrifices were worth it. I continued by explaining to the kids that when I let books lead me to think about big issues, I, too, often find myself left with more questions.

"Instead of raising questions and leaving it at that, however, I try to think through those questions. To do so, I return to the text and try to make more of the details. It is in the details that possible answers to my questions might be found.

"Today, I want to show you how I focus on characters as a way to think through my ideas. As I read," I told the kids, "I hold my thinking in my head and try to consider the way the characters' words, actions, and thoughts might contribute to my ideas. Watch how I do that as I revisit the part of 'The Lottery' in which the Hutchinsons 'win' the lottery." (See page 97.)

After thinking aloud and asking the kids to share what they noticed with their partners, I continued. "In this example, I focused on one particular character that I found compelling. I tried to think about Tessie Hutchinson. I considered why she acted the way she did and what this revealed about the kind of person she was. I did this for the purpose of stretching my thinking about the big questions I had raised about the text. I can think this same way about any or all of the characters in the text and can also think about how who they are is revealed in how they relate to one another. That's where we'll pick it up tomorrow. For now, let's just add to our ways of thinking that we can push ourselves to consider the kinds of people we are reading about as a way of making more of our ideas." Then I sent the kids off to read.

Making More of the Symbols in the Text

Once the kids saw that they could examine the details of characters' actions, words, and thoughts to think more deeply about the texts they were read-

Excerpt from "The Lottery"	Think-Aloud: Focusing on Character to Deepen an Idea
. . . there was a long pause, a breathless pause, until Mr. Summers, holding his slip of paper in the air, said, "All right, fellows." For a minute, no one moved, and then all the slips of paper were opened. Suddenly, all the women began to speak at once, saying, "Who is it?," "Who's got it?," "Is it the Dunbars?," "Is it the Watsons?" Then voices began to say, "It's Hutchinson. It's Bill." "Bill Hutchinson's got it." "Go tell your father," Mrs. Dunbar said to her older son. People began to look around to see the Hutchinsons. Bill Hutchinson was standing quiet staring down at the paper in his hand. Suddenly, Tessie Hutchinson shouted to Mr. Summers, "You didn't give him enough time to take any paper he wanted. I saw you. It wasn't fair."	Mrs. Hutchinson seems to be one of those people who cries foul when things don't go her way. She says it's not fair, but this has been going on for years. Also rememember, she was the one who almost forgot what day it was and came rushing up late. Perhaps she considers it a sacrifice worth making until it's her family.

ing, I wanted to help them see other details of their texts as symbolic. This idea was challenging because kids often see literary symbolism as a secret they are either privy to or not. I wanted to help them see that there was no secret here. I wanted them to know that understanding symbolism involved a habit of mind that they could develop. I wanted to teach them that as they read and began to explore issues in their reading, they could consider the details of the text as symbolic of something connected to the issues.

Typically, to teach this idea, I would demonstrate for kids how to turn the details of their texts into symbols. This year, however, I had Beth in my class. Beth was one of a small number of students somewhat skilled in making symbols of the details. I realized this from looking at book talk preparation work she had done after I had read aloud Joyce Carol Oates' "The Visit" (1993) one day in class. Because this was a shared text for the class, Beth's work was a particularly lucid example of a new way of thinking for the class. So I simply copied her work onto overheads and talked to the students about how they too could try to make symbols of the details of their reading.

"Remember when we read 'The Visit,' the short story by Joyce Carol Oates about Lisanne, who resisted visiting her grandmother in the Alzheimer's unit of the hospital? The story takes place on a day in which Lisanne succumbs to her mother's pressure to visit her grandma and is transformed by the experience. Many of you were talking about how the story seemed to position us to think that it's fear of the unknown that makes us avoid doing things. But you left it at that. Well, when I was looking through the writing in your literacy notebooks from that read-aloud, I noticed that a couple of you took that idea further. Today, I want to share with you Beth's work because the way she went further involved a new kind of thinking that all of you could be doing."

Beth's Thoughts from "The Visit"

Her grandmother used to keep roses and they mostly flourished greatly, but the ones that didn't were overrun with spots and Japanese beetles. The roses are memories to her grandmother. The beetles tainted the roses, just as the Alzheimer's tainted her memories. There are no roses in the garden in the hospital because it would hint at what's missing to the residents.

Perhaps Lisanne's coming to visit and talking to her grandmother represents a return of the roses. Lisanne recognizes this as she talks to her grandmother and sees her differently. This makes her less afraid. When Lisanne gets over her fear of the hospital she represents a return of beauty and memory to her grandmother's life.

I continued, "I want you to notice the way that Beth tried to make more of the details of the story by turning them into symbols. This allowed her to think about the ideas in the story in new ways. By seeing the memories as tainted, and seeing Lisanne as representing a way to heal, Beth was able to think about the power that comes from overcoming our fears.

"You, too, can make symbols of the details of your story. Over the next couple of days, I want to focus on this sort of thinking by looking at the kinds of details that are worth thinking about. Let's start by just opening our minds to the idea of symbolism in and of itself."

Over the next few days, I taught lessons that were intended to help the kids turn the details of their books—the colors and names and recurring objects or places—into symbols. Moreover, I showed them how to pause and consider the significance of these symbols as a way to imagine new and surprising ideas about their texts and they ways the texts positioned them to think about their lives.

Developing an Interpretation Across a Text

As a general rule, my students do very little writing about reading. They do not regularly write summaries of the reading they do for homework. I do not require them to write a particular number of sticky notes for each book. They never write book reports. I find that too much emphasis on writing takes away from their reading. My goal is to ensure that the kids spend most of their reading time actually reading. Additionally, when kids write about reading, if there is no audience for the writing, it is often thoughtless and of poor quality.

There are times, however, when a little writing about reading does help. When I want to show the kids how they can hold onto a thought or linger on an idea, I introduce them to some writing strategies. Sometimes, when we are in the midst of a whole-class reading inquiry (for example, trying to consider the ways books position us to think about big issues), I ask the kids to jot down some ideas so that we, either as a class or in conferences, can look at our thinking and try to stretch or revise it.

So that the writing never takes over our reading time, I always begin with sticky notes. I gathered the kids in the meeting area for a minilesson in which I start by passing around a bunch of large sticky notes.

"Over the past few weeks, we've focused on two seemingly discon-nected ideas. One is to make more of the details of the books we are read-ing. The other is to think about how the books we are reading position us to think about large issues. I've noticed that instead of gathering up your thoughts about the details of the text and letting each contribute to the way you think about a small number of very big ideas, many of you are turning each of the details into big issues and developing lots of small thoughts about really big ideas. Today I want to show you how to use your Making More thinking to develop your big issue thinking. I have been working with Jer-emy on this idea in our conferences, so I've got his work here on an over-head as an example."

I showed the kids how Jeremy placed a sticky note at the halfway point in the book and at the end of the book. "When we read," I explained to the kids, "we spend time at the beginning of the book trying to focus on our thoughts and opinions of the details of the text. By the time we get to the middle, we are ready to stop and consider issues the author might want us to explore. To push ourselves to really consider these issues, we need to stop reading the book and go back to the beginning—to reread all our sticky notes, trying to name the issues that are hiding in the text. Then we can jot our thinking on the middle-of-the-book sticky note. Notice the way Jeremy did this on his middle-of-the-book sticky.

The Winter Hare, **by Joan Goodman (1996)**
Halfway Sticky Note
What issue does this text explain?
  This text is about power. Power itself enslaves many people to do things in order to get it, whether by sneaking or purposely doing things to others. The power-hungry people do anything to get it regardless of who they affect. To them it's all worth it. The people who see that power [is] still too far from reach do what they can honorably to grab power!

"This forces us not to just let the ideas float around in our heads but to actually develop words to talk about them," I explained. "This slows us down and holds us accountable for really thinking about the issues. Then as we read on, we carry the idea in our heads and think about how it develops across the book. When we get to the end, before we return the book to the shelf, we take a little time to reconsider the idea we've developed and jot our new thinking on the end-of-the-book sticky note."

The Winter Hare, **by Joan Goodman (1996)**
End-of-Book Sticky Note
What does this text do to indulge the issue?

The text shows that people who have power do not feel it is enough. They get addicted to needing more power and do not allow people to get in their way. In the long run, it shows that the power-hungry people do not achieve what they want. The people who strive for respect end up on top.

I closed the lesson by asking the kids to each take two sticky notes and place them in their books. I told them I expected them to begin this work by using the strategy as I'd shown it to them and then, over time, invent their own ways to name their thinking while reading and push it further.

Resisting the Text

After teaching quite a number of lessons that asked kids to make more of the details of their books and use them to develop interpretations, I noticed an interesting issue. Sometimes kids were misunderstanding the texts they were reading and not recognizing that they were doing so. I noticed it first when I was sitting in a social studies class. The kids were in the midst of a unit on women's history and women's rights in America and on this particular day, they were reading a chapter from Penny Colman's *Girls: A History of Growing Up Female in America* (2000). As they worked through the chapter, I noticed that many of them were shifting the meaning of the text. For example, the text said, "In Western societies, the female gender role is usually described as nurturing, expressive, cooperative, and sensitive to the needs of others. The male gender role is described as independent, aggressive, dominant and ambitious." The kids read that as "Girls are nurturing, can express themselves, cooperate, and are sensitive. Boys are independent, pushy, and want to be successful." I wondered for a while what made them interpret the text in that way. After all, it wasn't that they didn't know what the word *described* meant. After some consideration and a search for similar instances during independent reading, I came to understand that many of the kids transformed texts quite possibly because they resisted the ideas that were presented there.

In an attempt to make sense, readers often turned the words into what they expected them to say. These readers had notions about the world that they were holding onto as they read. And even when a text tried to challenge those notions, the readers held tight.

It was difficult to imagine how to help the kids see this. After all, they did not know they were miscuing. I decided to begin by simply opening their minds to the possibility that when they read, they might be shifting the meaning of the texts out of resistance to the ideas. To do this, I put a page of the Colman text on the overhead along with two example retellings of the text. I told the kids that earlier in the week, as I was sitting in their social studies class watching them work with this text, I noticed that many of them were misinterpreting the text without realizing they were doing so. "This is hard to combat sometimes," I continued, "because the reason you're struggling to explore the thinking in the text is because the ideas in the text are ones you resist. You don't quite agree with them, so you change the text into what you need it to be." I told them to look at the two retellings (see page 103) and talk to their neighbors about how each retelling changed the meaning.

After talking to her partner for a couple of minutes, Iyana raised her hand. "I get what you are saying, Donna, but how do you know when you've changed the meaning? I mean, if you make it into what you want it to say, then you think that's what it says. How do you know it's wrong?"

"Great question. That's the hard part. Usually you can tell that something's awry when you read on. Often when you misinterpret a text, later parts don't make sense. Remember, each part of a text connects to the parts that came before. So if you read on and become confused, you need

Actual Text	Student Saying the Text So That It Makes Sense	Donna Saying the Text So That It Makes Sense
In Western societies, the female gender role is usually *described as* nurturing, expressive, cooperative, and sensitive to the needs of others. The male gender role is *described as* independent, aggressive, dominant and ambitious.	Girls *are* nurturing, can express themselves, cooperate, and are sensitive. Boys *are* independent, pushy, and want to be successful.	Girls *are seen as* nurturing, able to express themselves, cooperative, and sensitive. Boys *are seen as* independent, pushy, and driven to succeed.

to go back in the text and ask yourself whether there are parts for which you need to revise your understanding. Tomorrow, I'll put up more of this text and show you what I mean. We'll look at a misreading and how if you hold onto it, you'll get confused later."

The next day, I put up a much larger chunk of the text and thought aloud in front of the kids, holding onto a misreading until I hit a part that confused me. Then I showed them how to go back and reconsider the meaning of earlier parts by looking at word choice.

Step Back and Reflect

No matter how many times I teach the same thing, or how diligently I prepare for contingencies, I am always surprised at how different kids by nature will react differently. Each year, there comes a point when I am reminded that I teach human beings who don't always respond the way I hope and expect. When those times come, I am often tempted to shift my goals or lower my expectations.

Helping kids buy in to new ways of thinking about reading is very challenging. It requires a shift in thinking that I struggle to help the kids recognize. Learning to explore the kinds of questions that help us read books critically and to use books to read the world more critically often feels outside of the experience and ability of my kids. Their responses feel stale and cliché—so much so that I am tempted to lead them through the thinking. I am tempted to ask them specific questions about their books that will lead them to more critical thinking.

Instead, however, I need to hold onto my fundamental belief that the only reason to teach any habit of mind is so that kids will learn to self-initiate it in their own lives. Therefore, I need to teach them to ask and grapple with critical questions themselves. If I continually remember this goal, then I allow myself the space to let kids respond to their reading in ways that might seem stereotypical to me but represent new thoughts for them. At the same time, then, I can plan to angle my next units of study toward deepening their thinking and understanding of critical perspectives.

Think About Your Classroom

◆ At points during the year, kids will resist the curriculum. Don't let that deter you. Your dreams and goals for your class are important. Don't be afraid to stay the course.

◆ Help kids understand that using reading to explore big issues in the world involves a particular habit of mind. Remember that that habit of mind needs to be explicitly taught.

◆ Begin by helping kids understand that there are issues hiding in the texts they read. Demonstrate for kids how to name those issues by looking at a familiar text together and sharing your thinking with them.

◆ Teach kids that there's more to developing an interpretation than naming the issues hiding in their texts. They should also think about the ways the books they are reading position them to think about those big issues. Help kids understand that different texts position us to think differently about the same issues. You might teach this by looking at two texts that explore the same issue and thinking aloud for them how the texts position you to think differently.

◆ Spend some time teaching kids that they can make more of the details in a text and use those ideas to develop their interpretations. You might teach them how to make more of the characters' names or the places in which the stories are set. You might also teach them to make symbols of the details of the texts they are reading.

◆ If you notice in your research that kids are resisting the ways in which some texts are trying to disrupt their understandings or beliefs about the world, help them see their miscues and teach them how to reconsider their ideas about the texts.

Chapter 8

Finding Gray

Developing Justifiable Interpretations

"We have nothing else to say," Jazmin said as I sat down with her book club for a conference. It was mid-March and we had been in book clubs for about a month. The kids got into clubs soon after I had begun teaching them to explore the issues hiding in their texts. I decided to use clubs because they offer the opportunity for kids to examine and possibly extend or revise their thinking in the company of others.

When I pulled alongside Jazmin's club, they had in front of them copies of William Golding's *Lord of the Flies* (1954). There were also a handful of sticky notes in the middle of the table. "We just keep saying the same thing over and over again. It's boring," Jazmin continued.

"Exactly the same thing over and over again? You mean you just keep repeating the same sentence?" I asked. It may seem like a silly question, but I wanted to know what strategies they had tried to stretch out their ideas.

"Well, no, not exactly," Jason responded, "but we've tried everything to make our conversation longer and we just can't."

"What have you tried?"

"Well, we picked an issue—we picked leadership—and said how the text connects to it. We said that people become leaders either through fear or respect and we talked about parts that prove it, but now we have nothing else to say."

This was not new to me. Over and over again as I pulled alongside reading clubs, I heard the same thing. The kids felt as if they had nothing to say.

They had talked about parts of the story that were interesting to them, they had found issues they thought were hiding in the texts and even named ways the authors might have wanted them to think about those issues. And then they had become stuck. They couldn't seem to get into a discussion.

I, too, felt stuck. I listened to the conversations and they seemed shallow. It was like the kids were using the issues as ribbons with which to neatly tie up the books. The issues were ends, not means to new beginnings.

I found myself wanting them to go deeper into the texts, but I wasn't sure how to help them. My conferences seemed vague. The kids looked at me and nodded, but nothing really changed. So I decided to give myself some space to figure this out, and I took a two-day break from conferring. During that time, I did some research. I sat alongside club after club and tried to name as specifically as possible what they were doing and not doing so I could develop some lessons.

What I noticed was not very surprising. While the kids came to their clubs with a handful of possibilities, they tended to choose the easiest ones to talk about. It was as if they were taking their preconceived notions about an issue and just plopping them into the book. "This is a treat-people-the-way-you-want-to-be-treated book." Or "This is a people-who-have-power-do-anything-they-can-to-keep-it book." And when they talked they were mostly saying what they already thought. They weren't trying to make new thinking.

Finding the More Justifiable Interpretation

Helping students make new thinking from reading involved helping them fundamentally shift what they saw themselves doing as they developed interpretations of their books. Like Jazmin and her book club, many kids in my class still saw developing an interpretation as trying to come up with a quick answer to the book. This made them accept the first reasonable idea that was presented. I decided the best way to get kids to let go of mediocre ideas quickly and to be willing to rethink their own ideas was to name for them some beliefs about interpretation and to try to help them see new possibilities for their work.

I started with a minilecture as minilesson. I drew a line across a piece of chart paper that I had titled "Beliefs About Interpretation." On one end of the line, I wrote the word *one* and on the other, I wrote the word *any*. "Today I want to help you understand a little about the way different literary scholars and general readers think about interpretation so that over the next couple of weeks we can start working on developing stronger, more interesting interpretations of the books we are reading.

"Let's look at the line I've drawn on the chart paper. I often think about beliefs about interpretation as a sort of continuum. On one end," I said, pointing to *one*, "are people who believe that a story has one and only one correct interpretation. Some of these people believe that readers have only the words in front of them with which to develop it and others believe that you are supposed to know, by reading the book and perhaps by knowing a little about the author or the context in which the book was written, what the purpose for writing the book was, and this will inform your interpretation. Above all, however, there is only one right answer.

"On the other extreme," I said, pointing to the *any*, "are people who believe that a story has many interpretations and whatever you want to say about it is valid. You can have your opinion and I'll have mine. End of discussion.

"Both of these extremes are problematic," I explained. "Learning how to interpret is about learning how to negotiate. It's about trying out a bunch of ideas and grappling over which seems most interesting and convincing. It's about cracking open the details of the text and using them to imagine new responses to the text and to your life. If you get into the habit of trying to see things in newer, fairer ways, then you will do so in a variety of contexts in your community—now and when you are adults."

Next I drew a big *V* coming out of the middle of the line. "So toward that end, here's where I want us to try to work—somewhere in the middle of these extremes, in a place I will call *the more justifiable interpretation*." I wrote those words on the chart. "I'll define the more justifiable interpretation as the one that is the most imaginative—that is, the one that pushes you to imagine new possibilities for the text and the world. It is the one that is most convincing. You talk about it in ways that compel others to join in on your thinking. And it's the one that is most accountable; that is, it takes into account significant parts of the text.

"Our goal as readers is to remember that we bring every bit of our identity and every one of our beliefs to our reading. In other words, the way we think about stories is affected by who we are. On the other hand, who we are and what we think is never an excuse to disengage from others. If we accept anything that someone says or dismiss it as just his or her opinion, we never learn how to rethink our own ideas and come to something new. Therefore, our job is to take the time to try out lots of ideas and to work together to figure out which is more justifiable."

Out of this talk, over the next couple of weeks, came a string of mini-lessons and conferences that were meant to help kids develop more justifiable interpretations. To begin, I offered them a set of guidelines for this work. I wanted to provide support that would hold them accountable for reaching for provocative ideas and would also bring together some of the ideas we had been exploring over the past couple of months.

I told the kids that I begin with simply naming the issues I think are hiding in the text I am reading. Then I try out each of the issues. That is, I try to think about what the text might be saying to me about each of these issues. Then I pick one that I think is most interesting and might help me imagine new possibilities for my world. Once I do that, I focus for a while just on this issue, thinking about how the text continues to position me to think about it.

To help them visualize what I meant, I put a chart (see page 110) up on the overhead.

Let me just underscore that I am often conflicted about using guidelines for thinking. I don't want a guidelines chart to become like a worksheet— a form the kids just fill out to say that they have completed their work. But I do think that guidelines charts are sometimes helpful in scaffolding kids as they develop a new habit of mind. When I decide to use them, I am very mindful of creating a transition through which the kids will stop using them, while continuing the thinking they supported.

What's most difficult about using guidelines charts, however, is finding a way to remove them without losing the thinking they supported. I find that

DEVELOPING JUSTIFIABLE INTERPRETATIONS—
SOME GUIDELINES THAT MIGHT HELP

Step-by-Step Guidelines	Examples from "Moonbeam Dawson and the Killer Bear," by Jean Davies Okimoto
First, *ask yourself*: What issues are hiding in this text? (This acknowledges that there is more than one issue.)	Well, this text seems to address the following issues: attraction/ adolescent love, family, masculinity, and environmentalism.
Then, *try out each of these ideas*: What is the text saying to me about each of these issues?	Attraction/adolescent love: kids will do anything for love family: we're influenced by families masculinity: boys lie environmentalism: caring about the environment is sometimes challenging
Then, *ask yourself*: Which of these is the most interesting? Which might help me imagine something new?	Masculinity is the most interesting one, so I'll stick with that.
Then, *ask yourself*: How does the text position me to think about this issue?	I think the text positions me to think that in the name of attracting someone, boys will put themselves in a situation where they get caught in a lie. They are afraid to not seem masculine or in the know. They don't want to seem weak, so they show off and then get caught in a lie.

this is often most easily done in conferences. One by one as the kids show an ability to move through the steps with ease, I replace the chart with other strategies. One involves more writing. Instead of having them use the chart to organize their thinking, I show some kids how to hold this line of thinking in mind and write it in paragraphs in their reading notebooks. I also tell the kids to use the middle-of-the-book and end-of-the-book sticky notes they learned about earlier as reminders to think. Many kids do that thinking on the sticky notes, but some leave the notes blank and find someone to listen to them talk through their thinking with when they reach the appropriate spot. When I see these conversations going on during independent reading, I jot a note in my conference notes and often listen in so I can keep track of the ways in which kids are holding themselves accountable to the work.

Expecting to Talk Longer

As kids' understandings about how to develop interpretations of their books shifted, I also came to realize that they needed some new ways to talk at length about these ideas. I am reminded of a speech Donald Graves gave at Teachers College last year. In arguing that kids need opportunities to talk long about their ideas, he challenged us to think about whether or not we provided those opportunities and helped kids think about ways in which they might lengthen their thinking (Graves 2003). I knew that I was providing the opportunities, but I hadn't really taught the kids how to stretch out an idea. I decided to start simply by helping kids have a vision—an expectation that they would use more words to describe what they meant. This vision needed to be concrete. I tried to think of an image of lots of words and, of course, paragraphs and pages came to mind. In conferences and whole-class discussions, I now find myself constantly asking the kids—and teaching them to ask each other—to talk in paragraphs and then pages of thought: "What you're saying is so interesting. I hadn't thought of it that way. Can you say that in three pages?" or "Try to add another paragraph of thinking."

Learning More About the Vocabulary of Conversation

Of course, along with providing kids with a vision for talking longer, I also needed to teach them a handful of language moves they could use to say more about an idea. To do this I gathered the kids in the meeting area and used a fishbowl strategy. I told the kids to listen to the conversation for examples of a particular kind of talk and jot them in their notebooks. I had them listen for examples of

◆ words we can use to stretch out an idea by describing what it is not

◆ ways to say the same thing with different words

◆ ways to stretch out an idea by saying what it is like

When everyone was ready, we began. For the first fishbowl, we talked about "The Blondfire Genome," a short story by Sean McMullen (1994) about a girl who buys into stereotypes because of jealousy and a desire for popularity. In the story, Megan is surprised to find that Jackie, the popular singer in an all-girl band, is interested in science.

Fishbowl Conversation

Ally: I want to talk about how this story both keeps stereotypes and breaks stereotypes.

Mark: What do you mean?

Ally: Well, in the story, Jackie's this cool, popular girl and she gets fired from the music group because she gets acne and then she gets interested in science.

Lily: So that's a stereotype. When she's popular, she's in a band and that makes her cool. But when she gets acne, she loses her spot in the band and is interested in science.

Mark: But she was interested in science all along. She was interested in science while in the band. She just gets a chance to spend more time on this interest once she gets kicked out of the band.

Ally: That's where it breaks stereotypes. Megan didn't expect Jackie to like science. Because all she saw was this beautiful girl singing and dancing around.

Mark: And she was surprised that Jackie liked science. It's like how people assume things about you because of how you look or what you do.

Lily: Yeah. It's like when you see someone beautiful on the street and you automatically think they must be a model or something.

Ally: I think the media makes us like that. I've never seen someone really cool and popular wanting to be a scientist or a teacher on TV.

Lily: The media puts out these images and we believe them.

Ally: Yeah, we don't look at them and say, "People aren't like that." We think, "That's the way it's supposed to be. If I want to be cool, I can't like science."

At the end of the conversation, I asked the kids outside the fishbowl to share what they noticed. They pointed to the first time Lily spoke as an example of saying the same thing using different words and the last time Ally spoke as an example of saying what something is not. This research into other people's conversations gave the kids the chance to see lengthened talk in action.

I also taught the kids that while there is language that helps conversation, there is also language that hinders it. Over the next few days, in our read-aloud discussions and book club conversations, I taught kids about this language using the following lessons.

Learning to Avoid Language That Hinders

"I agree with everything that's been said and . . ."

Often, when students use language like this, they are disregarding what's been said before as opposed to actually agreeing with it. They're just "playing the discourse game" so that they can say what they have been thinking about from the beginning. Rather than use language that muddies nuance and distinction, students should simply say that they want to add another idea to the conversation.

"You can have your opinion and I'll have mine."

While many students feel that this is a way to show respect for other's ideas, it actually undermines the group's ability to develop imaginative interpretations. When we position ourselves to accept anything that's been said as a way of being polite, we stop really listening to each other. We don't feel the need to be accountable to other ways of looking at the text or the world.

Further, this makes us less likely to negotiate with each other, and negotiation is essential for developing an interpretation. When we negotiate, we imagine others' ideas as our own and compare them with our initial thoughts. Thinking between ideas helps us discover new possibilities.

Of course, in the end, we might need to agree to disagree, but this should be a tool of last resort, not a place to begin.

Learning to Use Language That Helps

"I agree/disagree with the idea that . . ."

I want my kids to avoid saying, "I agree with so and so." Instead, saying, "I agree with the idea that . . . ," helps kids develop interpretations in two ways. First, it breaks down ownership of ideas. Once an idea is disconnected from a person, the group has more freedom to build it up or take it apart. Second, this language forces kids to rearticulate the idea that was introduced. This confirms and clarifies understanding for the speaker and the group. So often in the classroom we are afraid of repetition. We think this means that kids aren't listening. But repetition used well can help kids try out ideas that aren't their own.

"I see it slightly differently."

Often kids get stuck when trying to explore ideas together because they ignore differences in each other's ideas. They don't listen for nuance. Listening for differences in their ideas helps kids reach new depths in thinking and develop subtle, richer understandings.

Language prompts are a good way to avoid problems in discussions. When kids use either of the following prompts, they are opening up an interpretation to examination and negotiation.

"I wonder how the part about . . . fits in."

When kids see their work as simply finding parts to support generalizations, they tend to disregard whole chunks of texts. While I want to teach kids to linger on parts and develop richer inferential thinking around them, I also want them to look for broader ideas. This requires consideration of more of the text and finding ways to support or critique a thesis with text that doesn't fit as well.

"Maybe there's a more imaginative way to think about it."

When students define interpretation as finding the one big idea or the author's message, they tend to make cliché statements that act as a sort of ribbon with which they can easily tie up a book. This will not lead to extended, deep, reimagined thinking about the text and the world. This is not to say that there are not plenty of valid interpretations, but only that kids are more likely to develop imaginative ideas if they're always positioning themselves *to reconsider* the ones they are working with.

Critical Questions That Extend Our Thinking

Once the kids had a handle on the kind of language that would help them extend their conversations, I tried to teach them that there were also predictable lines of thinking they might use to follow up on the thinking questions they had learned earlier. This is moving beyond just considering what an individual text wants us to believe; it involves learning to unpack the text and consider how these beliefs came to be and what the consequences of perpetuating them are. Therefore, after the kids could name an issue and think about the ways the text might have been positioning them to think about the issue, I taught them to stretch their ideas by trying to respond to any of the following:

- ◆ What might the writer believe in order to have written the text this way?
- ◆ What values or assumptions underlie this text?
- ◆ Is the way the text positions us fair or unfair?
- ◆ How does this text compare with others that explore the same issue?

- Who benefits from this thinking?
- Whose voices are missing from this text and how does that affect the telling?
- What could account for this idea? Where did it come from?
- What are the implications of this thinking? What are the outcomes?
- What are some alternatives to this thinking?

I taught these questions as a series of lessons in which I started with an idea we had developed in an earlier lesson and showed how to extend that idea using a new question as a guide. For example, one day, I returned to Beth's poem and put the following on an overhead.

Using Critical Questions to Extend My Thinking About a Big Idea
Internet Poetry, by Beth

First, I want to say again my original idea about the poem: Young people hide their true feelings even when they don't want to. Sometimes, in quiet ways, young people try to show their feelings, but when they are ignored, they hide behind a more acceptable identity.

Then, I want to push my thinking even further by asking, "What are the consequences of this thinking?" Perhaps what are considered normal ways of acting and feeling will never be challenged and those who think and feel in ways that aren't considered normal will always be othered.

I explained to the kids that people who read to develop their imaginations try to ask lots of questions to extend their thinking. I continued by telling them that it's not just any question, but a predictable set of questions that opens up new possibilities. "On the overhead is an example of one such question in action. Having developed an early idea about how Beth's poem positions me to think, I can extend that thinking by asking, 'What are the consequences of this idea?' That is, what are the effects of this idea living out in the world?"

To make sure the kids would try out this new question as well as the others I would introduce, I ended this and the next several lessons by asking the kids to turn to their neighbors and try out the question with their own independent reading.

Turning Ideas into Problems

As the kids developed more and more ways to think through the ideas they were raising in response to the books they were reading, I discovered something new. Despite previous lessons on making more of the parts of the text for the purpose of stretching an idea, I found that often the kids were using parts of the book for the purpose of simply supporting their ideas. Of course this wasn't necessarily bad. The fact that the kids felt they needed evidence to support their ideas meant that they knew they needed to be accountable to the text. The problem, however, was that using parts of a book only as supporting evidence kept the thinking small and made the kids avoid any critical examination of the issues the texts raised. Instead, the kids needed to see the parts of the text not as proof for theories they had developed, but as tools for exploration. Instead of just collecting up the parts, then, kids should have been unpacking them, examining the language used in the text for ways to develop their ideas.

Sondra was just finishing Laurie Halse Anderson's *Catalyst* (2002) when I pulled alongside her for a conference. She told me that the book had made her think a lot about outcasts. The book made her think that often kids' relationships change as the kids get to know each other more. In the story, Sondra explained, Kate and Teri weren't friends and even though Kate thought it was wrong for the kids at school to bully Teri, she never did anything about it. But then after a fire burned down her house, Teri started living in Kate's house. This gave Kate a chance to know Teri and therefore start to treat her better.

When she was done explaining this to me, Sondra paused, waiting for me to say something. I paused, too, wondering whether she would say anything else. After a moment of silence, I prodded a little. "So Sondra, what else are you thinking? You've got the beginning of an idea and have retold the story to me inside that idea. What will you do next to examine this idea?"

Sondra looked at me blankly, so I continued. "Well, one thing I notice, Sondra, is that to stretch out your idea, you retell the text. And while that's a good place to start, I want to suggest something more. I want to suggest that when you feel like you've got an idea figured out, one thing you can do is try to turn it into a problem. You can do that by turning back to the text and trying to let the exact words of the text make you question your early ideas. Let's try it a little together."

I then asked Sondra to find a section of the text that she thought connected to her idea. She turned to the part when Teri, the outcast, gets into a fistfight with the football team in the school cafeteria. In this part, Kate feels like she should do something for Teri, but she is conflicted. As Sondra and I reread the page together, we came across this line:

> This is the suburbs. With the exception of Teri Litch, no one knows how to throw a real punch.

I asked Sondra to pause for a minute. "Do you see this part?" I asked. "It's got me thinking about your idea. Earlier you said you thought Kate thought it was wrong for the kids to bully Teri, but she didn't do anything about it. When I read these two sentences, I see a possibility for your idea shifting. You see, these two sentences make me think that the text wants me to believe that suburban violence is not real violence. No one really gets hurt. It's not like in the city, where the real thugs are. It's just a case of kids being kids. We shouldn't worry about it. This part makes me begin to question Kate more—question her motives, her beliefs. And it makes me want to rethink your idea."

I finished the conference by suggesting to Sondra that she try to do the same thing as she kept reading. When she found herself developing an idea that felt finished, she could turn it into a problem by going back and rereading parts of the text that connected to her idea. When doing so, she would have to examine the language closely and be willing to see it in new ways.

Before I got up from the conference, I told Sondra that her classmates were working with their books in the same way she was and that the next day I would like to use her work as an example to share with the rest of the class. She agreed and promised to try to find another part of the text worth examining.

Maximizing Content Knowledge

Language and habits of mind alone are not enough to help kids expand their thinking. They also need to be able to bring outside content knowledge to their reading. Reading is a circular process. We read to know, but we also need to know in order to read. During an address at a National Council of Teachers of English convention some years ago, Maxine Greene spoke of how ideas are incomplete without information. A content-rich curriculum will

- ◆ immerse kids in studies that provide them with information that they can apply to their reading to make sense of it; reading is a way to come to know, but it also requires us to bring knowledge to it
- ◆ help kids develop the habit of mind to say to themselves that something unknown might be similar to something they know
- ◆ create in kids an interest in knowing more—in participating in group inquiries and developing independent interests

In my literacy class, I try to teach kids how to access the content knowledge they are developing in other classes and in their daily lives and use it to support their reading. Kids learn to ask themselves readerly questions like What do I know about the context in which this story is being told? and What is this like in the world that I know? Using these questions will help them make more reasonable sense of their books.

Kids need to be able to bring more to a text than what's literally there in order to think more deeply about their reading and their lives, but that does not mean they cannot or should not read books on topics about which they know little. You don't need to know everything about the Dust Bowl in order to read Karen Hesse's *Out of the Dust*. You don't have to know how genetic traits are passed from generation to generation in order to read

Kathryn Lasky's *Star Split.* In fact, that's the power of interpretation. We always have our own experiences and analogous events and concepts to help us make more. They might alter the experience, but they won't invalidate it.

But when kids don't have any sense of history or culture—a sense of the world outside of their own experiences—they do tend to dismiss what they don't know about or understand in a text.

For example, for many kids, American history skips from the Civil War straight to the Civil Rights movement of the 1960s. And they might be reading Mildred Taylor's *Roll of Thunder, Hear My Cry* not knowing much about what the American South was like for African Americans in the seventy-five or so years after the Civil War. I've met lots of kids who read that book and dismissed the context altogether. But kids who are immersed in a strong social studies curriculum, one that always tries to develop a sense of historical time, are probably more likely to raise questions about the context of this story and might even pick up a trade book on the subject in order to bring more specific understandings to their reading of the novel.

Additionally, kids who immerse themselves in inquiries, either independently or in a group (like a class), come to read with the expectation that there might be unknowns and develop ways to think about them. They might use analogous thinking or ask someone to explain or even look in another book for some answers to questions they have.

Getting Smarter About Concepts in the World

As we worked to try to lengthen our thinking about the ideas in the books we were reading, it became increasingly clear that the kids' limited understanding of the issues they were exploring in the texts was holding them back the most. Even after having learned ways to stretch out their ideas, kids still couldn't come up with well-developed ideas about any of the concepts. For example, when they talked about gender, they would say that girls were once discriminated against but now are equal to boys, but they had difficulty examining the issue further. They had a hard time thinking about how gender roles are created and didn't look at their own daily experiences so they could talk about how gender roles continue to be played out in ways that are discriminatory.

I knew that if I wanted to help the kids read with greater sophistication and to use their reading as a tool to live more actively and responsibly, I had to create an opportunity for them to get smarter about these ideas and then teach them ways to bring their new understandings to their reading. I hoped this would help them develop more complex ways of thinking about these issues (Bomer and Bomer 2001).

I began by collecting as many texts as I could—long and short—that explicitly dealt with the issues I wanted the kids to think more about. I decided to focus on those that most often came up in class in stereotypical ways. Therefore, I searched for texts on race, wealth and poverty, gender, and adolescent development. I searched for informational texts and essays that explicitly explored these ideas. Even more so, I found texts that explored the same ideas from different perspectives and texts that discussed different aspects of the same ideas.

For example, to help the kids deepen their thinking about wealth and poverty, I pulled out two articles from *Upfront* magazine, one on poverty in America and the other on the Enron scandal and set them alongside excerpts from Meredith Bagby's book *We've Got Issues* (2000) and Barbara Ehrenreich's *Nickel and Dimed: On (not) Getting by in America* (2001). To extend their thinking about gender issues, I copied a *New York Times Magazine* cover story from a couple of years ago on "mean" girls and a *Newsweek* article that followed and was written in defense of "good" girls.

Over the following few weeks, the kids spent some of their reading time working with these materials. They did so in partnerships in much the same way they had read short stories earlier in the year. That is, they sat hip to hip with one copy of the text between them. As they read silently to themselves, they talked to each other, trying to make the texts make sense. To push themselves to read in ways that would expand their understandings of these issues, at the end of each reading they reviewed the text and wrote on an index card something new they found in the text, something they had never thought of before. They then posted these index cards on bulletin boards dedicated to these issues. This simply enriched their understanding of these ideas.

In addition, once a week the kids got into conversation groups to talk about the issues. The purpose of these discussions was to try to dig into the messy parts of these ideas. I wanted the kids to grapple with what are often contradictory beliefs and values surrounding these issues. To prepare for these discussions, the groups gathered around the bulletin boards they had created and reread them, searching for two or more seemingly contradictory ideas. This was meant to develop complexity of thought. I defined *complexity* as the ability to hold in your mind two seemingly contradictory ideas and try to reconcile them. Once they had the ideas written down, they found a quiet spot in the room to do some freewriting for the purpose of getting their minds really going on the ideas. After about ten minutes or so, they gathered in their groups to discuss the ideas.

Searching for complexity in the bulletin boards immediately changed the way kids talked about these issues. Instead of repeating different versions of "Discrimination is bad; you shouldn't discriminate," kids began taking up harder ideas with regard to race, gender, class, and age. Some groups discussed how people sometimes internalize their own discrimination and end up contributing to it. Others talked about whether or not society has a responsibility to make sure people can live healthy, safe lives and what our individual role is in that responsibility.

The conversations got hard, too. The act of finding contradictions in the ideas immediately put the kids in the position of having to talk about really difficult and sometimes sensitive issues that cut to the heart of their experiences and value systems. Too often, however, when the issues got personal, the discussions turned into "talk the talk" discussions. The kids would wax poetic about these beautiful ideas that they never lived up to. Middle schoolers, like many of us, are famous for saying one thing and doing another. This kind of character education, in which we help the kids search for complexity across their reading and then teach them to talk through that complexity, can make them face hypocrisy in their own lives and possibly alter their beliefs or behavior, if they let it.

For example, Louis was known for saying one thing in class and doing something else in the schoolyard. One day I walked over to his group while he and a couple of his groupmates were going on and on about how mean it is to call people names and to use sexuality as a way to hurt others. Across the table was Teddy, silent Teddy, who probably no more than an hour before had been victim to Louis' name-calling. Yes, Louis had been one of a handful of people who had been flinging the word *faggot* at Teddy and here he was talking about how people shouldn't do it, and worse than that, no one was calling him out on it. For the purpose of trying to help the kids use the ideas in their reading as tools to imagine new ways of thinking and *acting*, I decided to jump in.

"I'm going to join your conversation for a bit, " I told the kids, "just to show you some ways to raise the stakes in your talk. OK?" I sat down, listened a little longer, and then said, "I'm sitting here listening to you and I can't help but think about whether or not what we say matches how we act. For example, you're talking about how it's wrong to call someone names and I think so too, but I can't help but admit that I have sometimes done it. I have sometimes called someone a name and then also said it's wrong. And I'm wondering whether any of you do it, too. I'm wondering, do any of us around this table sometimes even use the word *faggot* to hurt or get called *faggot* as a weapon against us? Maybe we could talk about when and why we do it even when we know it's not OK. Maybe this conversation would deepen our understanding about these ideas. "

Needless to say, the group got pretty quiet for a few moments. It wasn't a secret. Everyone knew that Louis had bullied Teddy. And then after a few moments, Louis admitted it. He said, "I have. I've called Teddy a faggot." And luckily we all waited. No one attacked or made excuses or fired hard questions back at Louis. We just waited for him to say more. "I'm not really sure why I do it. Maybe it's because I'm afraid of being attacked by others, so I act mean to people sometimes."

And then Angel added, "And maybe the reason you say it's not right when you're sitting here is because it's kind of safe practice. You know, if you say it's wrong a lot, maybe you'll convince yourself not to act mean next time."

When I got up from the group, I wondered if I had gone a bit too far, calling them to task—Louis in particular—the way I had. But I also knew the discomfort and difficulty were worth it. If we don't get to the really uncomfortable parts, the lessons about reading shifting our values and actions will always stay on the surface, like slogans we might find on posters in an educational store.

Bringing Complexity to Independent Reading

At the same time that the kids were reading about and discussing these ideas, I continued to confer during independent reading and book club meetings. I was interested in how the kids were starting to bring new, more complex understandings to their reading and group discussions. I was especially interested in their ability to see contradictions in their thinking and their attempts to work through them.

One morning, I pulled alongside Andy as he was reading Jerry Spinelli's *Loser* (2003). I began the conference they way I begin most, by asking him to talk to me about some of the thinking he had been doing as he read.

"Well, I'm reading *Loser* and I read *Stargirl* [Spiinelli 2002] before that. I've been thinking a lot about kids who are different and how people treat them. I see a lot of people getting made fun of for being different. And so I'm thinking about that as I read."

"Can you talk about how the book is getting you to think more about this idea?"

"Well, I'm thinking that I would never want to be friends with Zinkoff. He's just so weird. Who would want to be friends with someone like that?"

"What do you mean?" I asked. "Can you talk for a couple of paragraphs of thinking?"

"He does all these weird things. The kids don't like him. It's like Stargirl. The kids think she's strange. They're mean to her because she's different. I don't think they should do that. Just because someone's different, you shouldn't be mean to them."

As Andy talked, it seemed as if he did not see the conflict in his thinking. I decided to respond by repeating back to Andy what he had said to see if he could recognize it. "So you're saying you wouldn't be friends with Zinkoff because he's weird, but kids shouldn't be mean to Stargirl because she's different? Am I getting that right?"

"Yeah." Andy paused a bit and then continued. "Not being friends with someone who's different is not the same as being mean to them, I think."

I smiled at Andy. "It seems as if you have an issue here that you can use the book to work through for yourself. It's pretty challenging to think about what it means to treat someone badly. Is rejecting someone as a friend the same as being mean? This is such powerful reading work for you to be doing and also great life work. As you read on, you need to carry this new idea into the book and look for places where you can add more to your thinking. You probably want to put some reminder stickies in the book to hold yourself accountable. I know you'll also figure out some way to let the thinking you're doing affect the way that you look at kids around you—your friends and classmates. I'll ask you about it in our next conference. I look forward to hearing what you have to say."

Step Back and Reflect

As I walked away from my conference with Andy, I was reminded of the potential power of this work. Through his reading and his thinking between the two Spinelli books, Andy was beginning to develop the kind of imagination I was teaching toward. When Andy said he was thinking a lot about kids who are different, he was placing these stories in the context of larger ideas. When he said he saw a lot of people getting made fun of for being different, he was recognizing that these ideas were not just hiding in the books but also in the world in which he lived. When he said that he would never want to be friends with Zinkoff and that he thought kids shouldn't be so mean to Stargirl, he was seeing them as real people that he could know and was imagining a response to them. And when awakened to the potential conflict between those last two ideas, he opened himself up to a problem worth grappling with.

And while I am excited by the fact that Andy, along with many of his classmates, is finding his way through these ideas, I am also reminded of how hard it is to teach kids that reading can give us the power to act and can therefore change the situations in which we find ourselves. This learning takes time and requires constant opportunities to try out our thinking and question others. I still struggle to ensure that kids have these opportunities and grapple with the reality that the effects of these lessons often feel a long way off.

Think About Your Classroom

◆ When kids' book discussions appear to be floundering, don't lose heart and don't think "It's not working." Instead try to see student struggles as opportunities for new instruction. Turn these problems into research. Begin by listening hard to what kids are doing and trying to name what's missing from their talk.

◆ Kids often see interpretation as coming up with an answer to the book—a singular message. While there are many valid interpretations of a text, try to teach kids to resist their search for the one message of the book by trying to reach for the most imaginative idea worth exploring in the book. Help the kids understand that they have to try out a number of ideas, not just go with the first one they think of.

◆ Kids need explicit lessons in the language they can use to stretch their minds. Notice the language they use that opens up conversation and the language they use that shuts it down. Teach them to use phrases like "I agree with the idea that . . ." and "I see it slightly differently" and "Maybe there's a more interesting way to think about it." Have them avoid phrases like "I agree with everything that's been said and . . ." and "You can have your opinion and I'll have mine."

◆ Figure out whether your kids are applying overgeneralized understandings of complex concepts to their reading. That is, are they relying on stereotypes about big issues like race, class, gender, and so on? If so, you might create a context for kids to read, write, and talk about big ideas from a variety of perspectives so that they can bring more complex thinking to their reading. You might gather readings or short clips from films that explicitly address these ideas and provide opportunities for the kids to read, view, and talk about them.

....

CHAPTER 9

Turning Hope into Action

I often worry that much of what I'm teaching falls into a category of work that I have sometimes called the hoped-for curriculum. That is, I teach lots of lessons about the idea that reading can challenge our view of the world. And I demonstrate the strategies and habits of mind that I believe will support the kids in thinking and acting more critically. And then I *hope* that those lessons will take hold and translate into action on their part.

When I was a new teacher, struggling to figure out whether my students were growing as readers, a school psychologist told me that all I could really do in my class was plant seeds. But, he said, I could never really expect to see the fruits of my teaching. I could only hope that if I planted enough seeds, years from then, in a time and a place I wouldn't know, former students would access what they had learned in my room and it would help them succeed.

But planting seeds and hoping that they sprout is not enough. In fact, it's irresponsible. And even though self-initiated critical thinking and action in response to reading is hard to see in the confines of a classroom, I have to find ways to make it more visible.

In Chapter 2, I outlined a number of ways that I assess students' developing understandings of the reading ideas we explore together. I discussed conferring as my primary assessment tool but also described literacy notebooks, newsprint charts, sticky notes, and book talks as ways to see what kids are understanding and able to do as readers. But, despite all of this, the evidence that kids have let reading lead them to action—to stand up to their friends or treat someone more thoughtfully or negotiate a more responsible decision—is still mostly unavailable to me. It typically materializes outside of reading time, when they're living their lives.

Sometimes, however, it pops up in the classroom in the most unexpected times and we can miss it if we're not paying attention.

Opening My Eyes to Self-Initiated Social Action in Response to Reading

When terrorists rammed airplanes into the World Trade Center on September 11, 2001, my students and I were starting our fourth day of school two blocks away. That morning, when kids were just getting to know their teachers and reacquaint themselves with their classmates, they were thrust into a nightmare that had the potential to break the best of us. And while all of our kids rose to the challenge of the day, holding hands as they walked up the West Side Highway after having been told to evacuate the building, sharing cell phones to try to contact families, and quietly comforting each other during the long wait at the elementary school to which we had been sent, the following months were powerfully challenging.

Told we would not be able to return to our school for quite a bit of time, my colleagues and I and our three hundred students moved into an already overoccupied school building on West Seventeenth Street. The O'Henry Complex was then home to two schools and the district's program for failing eighth graders. We became the third school crammed into the same building.

Despite the incredible generosity with which the teachers of the O'Henry building opened up their school to us, these were trying times. For the first few weeks, our kids stayed in the same classroom each day and teachers moved from room to room. I taught with only what I could carry around in a backpack and a crate. Having left their brand-new notebooks in their backpacks and lockers back at our school, my kids had none of their supplies and were left to either repurchase everything or wait for the donations that eventually arrived from around the country.

Classroom libraries, made up of books donated from friends at the Teachers College Reading Project and countless teachers across the country, were limited and set up in three rooms—not necessarily the ones in which my colleagues and I were teaching literacy at any given time. Often kids had to leave the classroom and interrupt a science class or a math class to find a new book.

While most of us tried to keep a stiff upper lip, it was becoming increasingly difficult. The rhythms of life at my school, especially the after-school routines the kids had come to value most deeply, were interrupted. Intermediate School 89 is one of a number of choice schools in our district. Families of fifth graders spend a significant part of the fifth-grade year touring and applying to the middle schools of their choice. This means that most of our kids do not come from the immediate neighborhood, but from all parts of the district and city. Many kids travel anywhere between a half hour and an hour and a half on the subway to get to class. For the kids, this means strains on their after-school social lives. Kids cannot easily hang out after school at each other's homes or spend time together during the weekends without significant planning on the part of their families. This challenge gave rise to a very formal after-school culture for the kids. For example, each Friday, a large group of kids, with permission from their families, went to the movies together at the local theater in Battery Park City. In the wake of 9/11, these social systems were disrupted; the movie theater was no longer accessible and families were afraid to let their kids do anything after school except to come straight home. Needless to say, this contributed immensely to the stress kids were feeling.

Ultimately, all of this stress manifested itself in a culture of meanness that crept into the school. Kids were teasing and calling each other names. And while they often did so in the name of "just playing," it was made worse by the fact that the kids who participated did not see the problem they were creating. They saw only that they were all joking with each other. They teased only within their group. They didn't see that other kids in the class were intimidated, afraid to say the wrong thing for fear that they might become targets, and they didn't see that some of the perpetrators themselves were quietly hurt by it as well (a fact revealed in more than one family conference).

I decided it was time to take this conflict on and to do so within the context of the reading curriculum. I knew the power reading had to help us heal, to help us imagine possibilities for ourselves, so I began simply by investigating what was going on in kids' reading lives. I asked them to talk about what they were doing to find their way back to reading, and most said nothing. They were not reading. They simply couldn't focus on it. Most kids hadn't been able to do anything more than glue themselves to their parents' sides.

After a bit of silence, however, Tonya raised her hand. "I've been reading a bit," she told us. Of course, no one was surprised. Tonya was a prolific reader; she swallowed books. "I know, I know," she said, "I always read. But this is different. It's been hard for me, too, so what I've been doing is digging through my bookshelves for all the books I loved when I was little. I've stacked them on my nighttable and every night I read them over and over again. It helps me fall asleep."

Tamika raised her hand and said in almost a whisper, "Me too. I thought it was kind of stupid at first, but I have this collection of baby books and I started reading them to my little brother. He doesn't seem to care much, but I guess it kind of helps me."

And while a handful of kids had found some ways to get some reading back into their lives, still others continued to struggle. Leon raised his hand and said, "I'm not doing anything. I just can't. It's like, I try and then my mind wanders. I feel so guilty, I avoid the whole thing altogether." Many kids nodded in agreement.

This honest talk, about the real things we were doing as readers, even the talk about guilt, gave voice to every kid in the class. And our willingness to listen to each other and see commonality in our painful experience helped us heal.

Reading has always been a way for us to talk about hard issues as teachers. When trouble shows its face in our classrooms, we turn to books to help us open up discussion. In my class, talking about the reading itself became a way to talk about responding to chaos and terror. To talk about how we weren't reading was to share our nightmares, our distractions, our visions of future disasters. While these discussions began to help relieve some of the stress kids were feeling, the cruelty continued.

Then in late March, about two months after we finally returned to our building downtown, the unexpected happened. I begin reading aloud Nikki Grimes' book *Bronx Masquerade* (2002). It's the story of a group of high school kids in the Bronx who are studying poetry from the Harlem Renaissance in their English class. The study inspires one of the kids to write poetry, and an invitation by the teacher to read the poetry in class turns into a monthly and then weekly open-mike poetry session in which these guarded, have-to-save-face high school kids begin to unmask themselves.

One day, during my read-aloud, I read a part of the book in which Tyrone, whose role in the story is to act as respondent, talking back to each character's poetry, comments how a person just never knows how people feel about his or her words. He is responding to Janelle, who has just read her poem about feeling fat and ugly and wishing that people could see past what's on the outside. I found myself reading those words slowly again and again: "You just never know how people gonna feel." And each time I read them I set my eyes on the kids who controlled the culture of cruelty—Doug, and Brianna and Seth. A strange feeling came over the room, but it passed and we moved on, just letting the words of the book wash over us, not talking at all.

Two days later, after I had participated in many informal hallway chats about this meanness and after I had displayed the *New York Times* article on mean girls prominently in my room, I found a little sticky note stuck to my desk. It read, "Dear Donna, we want to stop the culture of cruelty. Will you meet with us to help us figure out how? Your students, Kyla, Maureen, Jana, Vanessa, and Ethan." I smiled. Of course I would help. I agreed to meet with them after school that Friday for a planning session.

As the meeting began, I found myself holding back a little bit. I simply listened to the kids talk, wondering whether or how much I should respond. Perhaps it would be inappropriate for me to share too much of my thinking about their behavior. As the conversation continued, however, I reminded myself that we always teach from our values and should not be afraid to do so. I shouldn't be afraid to tell the kids that change comes from the collective and comes from acting on your beliefs even when it's hard. I needed to teach them that they couldn't just get the bullies to stop on their own; they would get called stupid, baby, even bitch if they tried. Instead, the kids needed to get loud about it, loud enough so that others would hear and then join in to confront the bullies. They needed more and more kids to join their cause. I said, "Don't exclude others from any meetings that you hold. Invite them to be a part. The larger your side, the smaller theirs." I told the kids that they also needed to stop being friends with kids who were bullying. They were sending mixed messages by letting Donald call them a slut one day and letting him put his arm around them and whisper flirtations in their ears the next.

The kids agreed to try and over the next couple of days incredible things happened. During a read-aloud discussion, Maureen decided not to talk about what was happening to the characters in the book, but instead commented on how the book reminded her of our school and how it got her thinking about how we were acting toward each other. That comment led not only to a general discussion about bullying at school but to an all-out confessional where Seth stood up and apologized and then insisted that others apologize too. It could have turned into a little love fest then, but I decided to jump in. I told the kids it was good that some of them were apologizing and promising to change, but the real test would come the next day and the day after that when they actually would have to live out these promises.

Sure enough, not only did they try, but they also talked about it over and over again and looked for opportunities to deepen their thinking through their schoolwork. Kyla, Donald, and Nate built a text set around the issue of bullying as a book club. And at graduation, Donald gave a speech in which he said that one of the biggest impacts school had had on him that year was making him confront his bullying.

All of this is not to say that it takes great trauma to see the effects of a critical reading curriculum. In fact, that's a dangerous thing to believe. It's true that often the social change curriculum we teach is the one connected to times of chaos and disaster, but the fact is that change has the capacity to occur and does occur millions of times a day in response to the tiniest, most ordinary moments. Once I developed the eyes to see, I realized these moments were abundant. Dina came back to visit after her first few months of high school and the first thing she told me was that she had formed a Radical Readers Club. She explained that Radical Readers was a group of kids who got together on a regular basis to read and talk and take action based on the ideas they formed. I bumped into Jessie on the subway one day and she told me about the literary journal she was writing for and editing at her high school. She described it as a chance to put her thinking out in the world in ways that might get others to think. Curtis' mom told me of the films he was making and how he talked about just wanting to create stories that would grab people and make them think. I witnessed Jeremy outside during lunch one day picking up the garbage that others had left, remnants of their lunch. Mitchell became the youngest member of a corps of teenagers who were training to be peer sex educators through a program at a local community center.

Eric Booth, author of *The Everyday Work of Art* (1997), writes in his book about how we complain about the lack of responsibility in young people today. We constantly point to the many examples of dangerous language and behavior we see in kids and then we lay blame. Perhaps it's the media, technology, our overly busy lives that have created this irresponsibility. Booth, however, argues that more than anything else, this lack of responsibility comes from a lack of ability to respond. *Respond*, he reminds us, comes from the Latin word *respondere* and actually means "to promise." As teachers, we need to organize a reading curriculum that gives kids space to respond the way Booth suggests. That is, not just to react to something in our books—not just to retell or give our opinion or dismiss because we don't understand—but to actually connect and make a promise, a commitment to act.

And in the end, perhaps we just might help kids imagine a world for themselves and for those around them that's smarter, more caring, and more responsible than the one we are living in today.

Bibliography

BEERS, KYLENE. 2003. *When Kids Can't Read: What Teachers Can Do.* Portsmouth, NH: Heinemann.

BLAU, SHERIDAN. 2003. "Performative Literacy: The Habits of Mind of Highly Literate Readers." *Voices from the Middle* 10 (3): 18–22.

BOMER, RANDY. 1998. "Transactional Heat and Light: More Explicit Literacy Learning." *Language Arts* 76 (1): 11–18.

BOMER, RANDY, AND KATHERINE BOMER. 2001. *For a Better World: Reading and Writing for Social Action.* Portsmouth, NH: Heinemann.

BOOTH, ERIC. 1997. *The Everyday Work of Art.* Naperville, IL: Sourcebooks.

CALKINS, LUCY. 2001. *The Art of Teaching Reading.* New York: Addison-Wesley Educational.

DANIELS, HARVEY, AND STEVEN ZEMELMAN. 2004. *Subjects Matter: Every Teacher's Guide to Content-Area Reading.* Portsmouth, NH: Heinemann.

EDELSKY, CAROLE, ed. 1999. *Making Justice Our Project: Teachers Working Toward Critical Whole Language Practice.* Urbana, IL: National Council of Teachers of English.

FIELDING, LINDA G., AND P. DAVID PEARSON. 1994. "Reading Comprehension: What Works." In *Educational Leadership* 51 (5): 62–68.

FRIEDMAN, THOMAS. "Awaking to a Dream." *New York Times.* March 28, 2004.

GARDNER, HOWARD. 1991. *The Unschooled Mind: How Children Think and How Schools Should Teach.* New York: Basic.

ISER, WOLFGANG. 1974. *The Implied Reader: Patterns of Communication in Prose Fiction from Bunyan to Beckett.* Maryland: Johns Hopkins University Press.

KEENE, ELLIN OLIVER, AND SUSAN ZIMMERMAN. 1997. *Mosaic of Thought: Teaching Comprehension in a Reader's Workshop.* Portsmouth, NH: Heinemann.

LANGER, JUDITH A. 1995. *Envisioning Literature: Literary Understanding and Literature Instruction.* New York: Teachers College, Columbia University, and Newark, DE: International Reading Association.

MACKEY, MARGARET. 1997. "Good Enough Reading: Momentum and Accuracy in the Reading of Complex Fiction." *Research in the Teaching of English* 31 (4): 428–58.

PEARSON, P. DAVID, L. R. ROEHLER, J. A. DOLE, AND G. G. DUFFY. 1992. "Developing Expertise in Reading Comprehension." In *What Research Has to Say About Reading Instruction,* ed. J. Samuels and A. Farstrup. Newark, DE: International Reading Association.

ROSENBLATT, LOUISE. 1978. *The Reader, the Text, the Poem.* Cambridge, MA: Harvard University Press.

SERAFINI, FRANK. 2004. *Lessons in Comprehension: Explicit Instruction in Reading Workshop.* Portsmouth, NH: Heinemann.

SPIEGEL, D. L. 1996. "The Role of Trust in Reader Response Groups." In *Language Arts* 73: 42–49.

VASQUEZ, VIVAN. 2003. *Getting Beyond "I Like the Book": Creating Space for Critical Literacy in K–6 Classrooms.* Newark, DE: International Reading Association.

WIGGINS, GRANT, AND JAY MCTIGHE. 1998. *Understanding by Design.* Alexandria, VA: Association for Supervision and Curriculum Development.

WILHELM, JEFFREY D. 2001. *Improving Comprehension with Think-Aloud Strategies*. New York: Scholastic.

Classroom Texts

ANDERSON, LAURIE HALSE. 2002. *Catalyst*. New York: Penguin.

BAGBY, MEREDITH. 2000. *We've Got Issues*. New York: Perseus.

BLOOR, EDWARD. 1997. *Tangerine*. New York: Harcourt Children's.

————. 1999. *Crusader*. New York: Harcourt Children's.

BRADBURY, RAY. 1946. *Dandelion Wine*. New York: Doubleday.

BROOKS, MARTHA. 1994a. "The Tiniest Guitar in the World." In *Traveling on into the Light*, 1–11. New York: Orchard.

————. 1994b. "Where Has All the Romance Gone?" In *Traveling on into the Light*, 30–38. New York: Orchard.

COLMAN, PENNY. 2000. *Girls: A History of Growing Up Female in America*. New York: Scholastic.

CRONIN, DOREEN. 2000. *Click, Clack, Moo: Cows That Type*. New York: Simon and Schuster.

EHRENREICH, BARBARA. 2001. *Nickel and Dimed: On (not) Getting by in America*. New York: Henry Holt.

GOLDING, WILLIAM. 1954. *The Lord of the Flies*. New York: Penguin Putnam.

GOODMAN, JOAN. 1996. *The Winter Hare*. New York: Houghton Mifflin.

GRIMES, NIKKI. 2002. *Bronx Masquerade*. New York: Dial.

HANSEN, JOYCE. 2000. "A Safe Space." In *Lost and Found: Award-Winning Authors Share Real-Life Experiences Through Fiction*, ed. M. Jerry Weiss and Helen S. Weiss, 179–94. New York: Tom Doherty.

Jackson, Shirley. 1982. "The Lottery." In *The Lottery and Other Stories*, 406–12. New York: Farrar, Straus and Giroux.

Jones, Heather, et al. 2002. "What a Pizza Delivers." In *Nutrition Action Newsletter* 29 (5): 3.

Kerr, M. E. 1985. "Do You Want My Opinion?" In *Sixteen: Short Stories by Outstanding Writers for Young Adults*, ed. Donald Gallo, 93–100. New York: Bantam Doubleday Dell Books for Young Readers.

Lantz, Frances. 2003. "Standing on the Roof Naked." In *On the Fringe*, ed. Donald Gallo, 89–116. New York: Puffin.

McMullen, Sean. 1994. "The Blondfire Genome." In *Altered Voices: Nine Science Fiction Stories*, ed. Lucy Sussex, 67–84. New York: Scholastic.

Mori, Kyoko. 1993. *Shizuko's Daughter.* New York: Ballantine.

Myers, Walter Dean. 2000. "A Christmas Story." In *145th Street,* 105–16. New York: Random House.

Oates, Joyce Carol. 1993. "The Visit." In *Small Avalanches and Other Stories*, 287–310. New York: Harper Collins.

Okimoto, Jean Davies. 1989. "Moonbeam Dawson and the Killer Bear." In *Connections: Short Stories by Outstanding Writers for Young Adults*, ed. Donald Gallo, 15–27. New York: Bantam Doubleday Dell Books for Young Readers.

Paulsen, Gary. 1998. *Puppies, Dogs and Blue Northers: Reflections on Being Raised by a Pack of Sled Dogs*. New York: Bantam Doubleday Dell Books for Young Readers.

Peck, Richard. 1985. "Priscilla and the Wimps." In *Sixteen: Short Stories by Outstanding Writers for Young Adults*, ed. Donald Gallo, 42–6. New York: Bantam Doubleday Dell Books for Young Readers.

Rowling, J. K. 2003. *Harry Potter and the Order of the Phoenix*. New York: Scholastic.

Spinelli, Jerry. 2002. *Stargirl.* New York: Random House.

———. 2003. *Loser.* New York: Harper Collins.

Tauber, Chris. 2002. "Cells Allowed." In *Upfront* 134 (11): 7.

Taylor, Mildred. 1976. *Roll of Thunder, Hear My Cry.* New York: Puffin.

Testa, Maria. 1995. "Family Day." In *Dancing Pink Flamingos and Other Stories,* 45–54. Minneapolis: Lerner.

Tolstoy, Leo. 1976. *War and Peace.* New York: Signet Classics.

Waddell, Martin. 1991. *Farmer Duck.* Cambridge, MA: Candlewick.

Appendix: Short Text Collections

Short Story Anthologies

A Couple of Kooks, Cynthia Rylant

A Gathering of Flowers, Joyce Carol Thomas

America Street, Anne Mazer

American Dragons: Twenty-Five Asian American Voices, Laurence Yep

American Eyes: New Asian-American Short Stories, Lori Carlson

A Starfarer's Dozen: Stories of Things to Come, Michael Stearns

Athletic Shorts, Chris Crutcher

A Walk in My World: International Short Stories, Anne Mazer

A Way Out of No Way: Writings About Growing Up Black in America, Jacqueline Woodson

Bad Behavior, Mary Higgins Clark

Baseball in April and Other Stories, Gary Soto

Believing Is Seeing, Diana Wynne Jones

Coming of Age in America, Mary Frosch

Connections, Donald Gallo

Destination Unexpected, Donald Gallo

Doing Time: Notes from the Undergrad, Robb Thomas

Eight Plus One, Robert Cormier

Face Relations, Marilyn Singer

Girl Goddess Number Nine, Francesca Lia Block

Help Wanted: Short Stories About Young People Working, Anita Silvey

In the Land of the Lawn Weenies and Other Misadventures, David Lubar

Island Boyz, Graham Salisbury

Join In: Multiethnic Short Stories, Donald Gallo

Kissing Tennessee, Kathi Appelt

Leaving Home, Hazel Rochman

Lines in the Sand, Mary Hoffman

Local News, Gary Soto

Lord of the Fries, Tim Wynne Jones

Love and Sex, Michael Cart

Memories of Sun: Stories of Africa and America, Jane Kurtz

No Easy Answers: Teens Making Tough Choices, Donald Gallo

145th Street, Walter Dean Myers

On the Edge: Stories on the Brink, Lois Duncan

On the Fringe, Donald Gallo

Past Perfect, Present Tense: New and Collected Stories, Richard Peck

Period Pieces: Stories for Girls, Erzsi Deak

Places I Never Meant to Be, Judy Blume

Sixteen, Donald Gallo

Some of the Kinder Planets, Tim Wynne Jones

Stories from El Barrio, Piri Thomas

Sudden Fiction, Robert Shapard and James Thomas

The Book of Changes, Tim Wynne Jones

The Call and Other Stories, Robert Westall

The Color of Absence: Twelve Stories About Loss and Hope, James Howe

Thirteen, James Howe

Time Capsule, Donald Gallo

Tomorrowland: Ten Stories About the Future, Michael Cart

Toxic Love, Linda Holeman

Traveling on into the Light, Martha Brooks

Twelve Shots: Outstanding Short Stories About Guns, Harry Mazer

2041: Twelve Short Stories About the Future, Jane Yolen

Uncovered, Paul Jennings

Visions, Donald Gallo

What a Song Can Do: Twelve Riffs on the Power of Music, Jennifer Armstrong

What Are Your Looking At? The First Fat Fiction Anthology, Donna Jarrell
What's in a Name? Ellen Wittlinger
Who Am I Without Him? A Short Story Collection About Girls and Boys in Their Lives, Sharon Flake
Who Do You Think You Are? Stories of Friends and Enemies, Hazel Rochman
Working Days, Anne Mazer

Essays and Articles

A Summer Life: Short Essays, Gary Soto
Blue Jean: What Women Are Thinking, Saying and Doing, Sherry Handel
How Race Is Lived in America, Correspondents of the New York Times
Living Up the Street: Narrative Recollections, Gary Soto
"My Turn" (a weekly column in *Newsweek* magazine)
Small Wonder, Barbara Kingsolver
Starting with I, Youth Communication/Andrea Estepa and Philip Kay
Yell-Oh Girl: Emerging Asian American Voices, Vickie Yam

Magazines

Calliope (world history)
Choices (Science and health magazine by Scholastic)
Cicada (fiction and poetry)
Cobblestone (American history)
Cricket (various fiction)
Dig (archeology)
Explore (science)
Faces (world cultures and geography)
Footsteps (African American history)
Muse (science and discovery)
Odyssey (science)
Time for Kids (news and current affairs)
Upfront (*New York Times* newsmagazine for teens)

Index

"Christmas Story" (Myers), 48
class discussion
  about hard issues, 131–32
  agreement in, 113, 114
  cliché statements in, 115
  critical questions and, 115–17
  externalizing thinking in, x
  fishbowl demonstrations of, 45, 51, 112–13
  fitting parts of text into whole, 114–15
  getting started, 41–42
  group power and, 37–38
  language helping, 113–14, 126
  language hindering, 113–14, 126
  listeners and, 45
  newsprint charts and, 17–18
  opinions in, 113–14
  ownership of ideas in, 114
  personal connections and, 42–47, 51
  problems talking about books, 106–7, 126, 130
  quality of, 38, 45, 106–7, 111
  repetition of ideas in, 114
  research into, 38–42
  statements vs., 46–47
  strategies for, 21
  turntaking in, 38
  value of, 20
  on values and beliefs, 122–24
  vocabulary for, 111–15
classroom library
  limited, 129
  materials in, 8, 19
  organization of, 8
cliché statements, in class discussion, 115
Click, Clack, Moo: Cows That Type (Cronin), 92–94
clipboards, for conferences, 14–15
closing, reading workshop, 8–9
collaborative reading
  book clubs, 22, 106–7, 126
  partners, 21
Collins, Kathy, 45

Colman, Penny, 101–3
complexity
  in independent reading, 124–25
  in thinking, 122–23, 126
comprehension
  assessment of, 25–26
  attending to text, 53–64
  fluency and, 27
  packing details and, 54, 59–61, 64
  recognizing connection of parts of text, 54, 61–62, 64, 95, 114–15
  reflection on, 63–64
  retelling and, 27, 58–59
  saying text to clarify meaning, 54–56, 66, 102–3
conferences
  inferential thinking and, 82
  information collection in, 14–15
  instruction in, xi
  literacy notebooks and, 16
  in reading workshop, 8
  record sheets for, 8
  on retelling, 58–59
  reviewing notes, 15
  scheduling, 8
conflict, 129–30
connections. See personal connections
content knowledge, 119–20
contradictory ideas, 122, 124–25
conversation. See class discussion
Cormier, Robert, 16–17
criteria for rubrics, 14
critical questions, 115–17
Cronin, Doreen, 92, 93, 94
Crusader (Bloor), 48–49
curriculum
  hoped-for, 127
  social change, 132–33
  student resistance to, 104
  teacher research and, 35–36
  units of study, 9–10

Dandelion Wine (Bradbury), 49

ideas (*continued*)
  resisting, 101–3
  talking at length about, 106–7, 111
  turning into problems, 117–19
  writing about in literacy notebooks, 16–17
  writing on index cards, 121–22
imagination
  definitions of, 3–4
  developing, 3–4, 115–17, 125
  language use, 115
  reading and, 2, 4–5
inconsistencies, questioning, 31–32
independent reading
  books for, 8
  personal connections and, 47–50, 52
  in reading workshop, 7
index cards, 121–22
inferential thinking, 65–82. *See also* interpretation
  categories of, 75–76, 82
  defined, 69, 71
  demonstrating with think-alouds, 71–73
  Figure it Out inferences, 75
  importance of, 66–67
  language requiring, 69–70
  Making More inferences, 75–77, 95–96, 100, 105
  minilessons for, 67–73, 76–81, 82
  opening up idea of, 67–71
  questions for, 70
  reading and misreading patterns, 73–74
  recognizing shifts in time and place, 76–77
  reflections on, 81–82
  rethinking misunderstandings, 77–80
  student problems with, 66
  teaching, 65–67
intellectual work, xi
Intermediate School (I.S.) 89, xvii–xviii, 128–33
interpretation, 83–105. *See also* inferential thinking; justifiable interpretations

beliefs about, 108–11
  characters and, 95–96
  class discussion of, 21
  critical reading, 87–91
  developing, 99–103, 104–5
  fitting stories into categories, 32–33
  issues hiding in text, 87–92
  multiple correct views of, 108, 126
  personal connections and, 109
  putting pieces of text together, 95–103
  questioning inconsistencies and ironies and, 32
  reading thoughtfully, 83–87
  reflection on, 103–4
  resisting meaning of text, 102–3
  seeing books as end, rather than beginning, 33
  single correct view of, 108, 126
  symbols and, 96–98
  validity of, 108
intertextuality, 22
ironies, questioning, 31–32
irresponsibility, 133
Iser, Wolfgang, 81
issues. *See also* ideas
  characters and, 95–96
  difficulties discussing, 106–7
  hiding in text, 87–92, 104
  justifiable interpretation and, 109–11
  learning about, 120–24
  Making More inferences and, 100
  resisting, 101–3
  selecting books on, 121
  symbols and, 96–99
  thinking about in different ways, 92–94
  writing about, 99–101

Jackson, Shirley, 77, 95
justifiable interpretations, 106–26. *See also* interpretation
  complex thinking and, 122–25
  critical questions and, 115–17
  discussion vocabulary and, 111–15

newsprint charts, 17–18

Newsweek, 121

New York Times, 3–4, 131

New York Times Magazine, 121

Nickel and Dimed: On (not) Getting by in America (Ehrenreich), 121

9-11 Commission, 3–4

nonfiction, saying text to clarify meaning, 56–57, 102–3

note-taking, in reading conferences, 14–15

novels

  exploring social norms through, 81

  for read-alouds, 20

  whole-class reading, 24

Nutrition Action Letter, 56–57

Oates, Joyce Carol, 98

observations, recording, 35

O'Henry Complex, 128

Okimoto, Jean Davies, 46, 71, 110

open-ended questions, self-reflection with, 18

opinions, in class discussion, 113–14

"optimal books," 54

Orwell, George, 17

Out of the Dust (Hesse), 119

ownership, of ideas, 114

paragraphs, talking in, 111

parallel time cues, 77

parents, communicating with, 17

partnerships, for reading, 21

patience, sudent response to questions and, 49–50

patterns. *See also* misreading patterns

  inferential thinking and, 73–74

  looking for, in student reading, 35–36, 64

  of misreading, 28–33

Paulsen, Gary, 58

payoff, in reading, 50

Peck, Richard, 39, 55

personal connections, 37–52

  class discussion and, 38

  demonstrating value of, 43–44

  to each other's ideas, 44–46

  emotional, 39, 49–50, 51

  fishbowl discussions about, 45, 51

  in independent reading, 47–50, 52

  interpretation and, 109

  limited, 47–48

  marking with sticky notes, 48

  minilessons on, 51

  read-alouds and, 42–47, 51

  in reading, 11, 38–41, 47–50, 52

  reflection on, 50–52

  research, 38–42, 51

  retelling and, 40–41

  stretching ideas about story with, 38–39

  texts for, 51

  thoughtful, 48–49

place, recognizing shifts in, 76–77, 82

preconceived categories

  changing story to fit, 32–33

prior knowledge

  revising, 74

"Priscilla and the Wimps" (Peck), 39–44, 55, 65, 66

problems, turning ideas into, 117–19

proficient reading, demonstrating, 71–72

Puppies, Dogs, and Blue Northerns (Paulsen), 58

questionnaires, about reading habits, 23, 24

questions

  about issues, 96

  about reading, 23, 24

  critical, 115–17

  for inferential thinking, 70

  open-ended, 18

  patience and, 49–50

  "so what?", 48–49

  "What's the *that*?", 49–50

Radical Readers Club, 133

read-alouds
  group power and, 37
  personal connections and, 42–47, 51
  selecting, 20
reading. *See also* independent reading;
    texts
  assessing student attitudes toward, 23–24
  beyond the words on the page, 65–66
  bringing content knowledge to, 119–20
  characteristics of strong readers, 25
  envisioning through, 4
  fake, 23–24
  guiding concepts for, 10
  hard issues and, 131–32
  honesty about, 23–24
  imagination and, 2, 4–5
  learning through, 120–24
  between the lines, 25
  making new thinking from, 107–11
  with minds on, 73–74
  multiple levels of, 35
  payoff in, 50
  personal connections and, 11, 38–41, 47–
    50, 52
  purpose of, 81
  quality of, ix–x
  recording observations on, 35
  requirements for, 24
  social action and, 6, 127–33
  thoughtful, 4–5
  as transaction, xv, 63, 80–81
  as transmission, xv–xvi
  writing about, 99–101
reading conferences. *See* conferences
reading growth
  "Dear Donna" letters on, 18
  self-reflection on, 16, 18–19
reading materials. *See* texts
reading partners, 21
reading questionnaires, 23, 24
reading workshop, 6–22
  assessment, 12–19
  closing, 8–9

collaborative reading, 21–22
conferences in, 8
discussion, 20–21
independent reading in, 8
meeting area, 7, 8
minilessons in, 7–8
planning, 9
read-alouds, 20
reflection on, 22, 34
structures of, 7–9
units of study, 9–12
value of, 7
reality, imagination and, 3
recitation, retelling as, 29–30
record sheets, for reading conferences, 8
reflection. *See also* self-reflection
  on growth as readers, 16, 18–19
  on interpretation, 103–4
  on justifiable interpretations, 125–26
  on personal connections, 50
  on reading workshops, 22, 34
repetition, in class discussion, 114
rereading, 58
research
  into class discussion, 38–42
  curriculum and, 35–36
  habits of mind, xii
  personal connections and, 38–42, 51
research-based instruction, xii
resistance
  to curriculum, 104
  to text details, 101–3, 105
responsibility
  handover of, xi
  lack of, in young people, 133
responsiveness, 133
retelling
  comprehension and, 27, 58–59
  conferences on, 58–59
  demonstrating, 59
  engagement and, 29
  interrupting reading for, 58–59
  minilessons on, 59